# SEA EL SANTISIMO
## A Manual for Misa Espiritual & Mediumship Development

by Mario dos Ventos
Revised Edition, January 2008

**All rights reserved**

**Publisher:** Nzo Quimbanda Exu Ventania
**Printed:** Lulu Publishing
**ISBN: 978-0-9556903-0-3**
**Copyright Year:** © 2008, Mario dos Ventos

# SEA EL SANTISIMO
## A Manual for Misa Espiritual &
## Mediumship Development

by

Mario dos Ventos

**Nzo Quimbanda Exu Ventania**
*www.exu.moonfruit.com*
under the watchful eyes of the Maioral

# CONTENTS

## Novenas

## Some Other Prayers

# DEDICATION

*To Ramon*

*With deep admiration and in loving memory*

We pray that we shall play our part

in helping the eternal processes of creation,

to drive out the darkness, the ignorance, the superstition,

the selfishness, the violence and all that are hideous cancers

in your world.


Our task is to replace them with a sublime knowledge

that will enable the children of the Great Spirit to fill themselves
with the radiance that could be theirs.


In expressing our gratitude for all that we have received,

we pray that we may be worthy to continue

to be channels for this divine wisdom and power,

thus being able to serve others less fortunate than ourselves

and so help to strengthen and widen the spheres of influence

that can teach an increasing number of people

how to fulfill themselves.

## Niño de Atocha

**O** Most Gentle Child of God, listen to our supplications.
Holy Child of Atocha give us the dignity
of your presence in our homes,
guard us from divorce, indecent ways,
selfishness and all other vices unworthy of a spiritual home.
Grant many blessings to those who call upon you.
Open the gates so we may go through.
For this we pray.
AMEN

# INTRODUCTION

"Spiritism is a science which deals with the nature, origin and destiny of Spirits, as well as their relationship with the corporeal world."

Allan Kardec
(Taken from *Qu'est-ce que le Spiritisme? - Préambule*,
Translated from the original French)

## What is Spiritism?

In the introduction to *The Spirits Book*, Allan Kardec, the founder of modern day Spiritism, mentions that he has created the term 'Spiritism' to name the movement he was initiating because "*new things deserve new names*". But the exact origins of Spiritism are murky, as multiple movements contributed to the body of Spiritist beliefs and practices. As a religious establishment, Spiritism began with a French mathematician and scientist Allan Kardec, (born Hippolyte Leon Denizard Rivail) who developed an interest in the "spiritual manifestations" reportedly brought forth by spirit, mediums- table tapping, apparitions, phantom music, and other phenomena attributed to the actions of spirits attempting communications with mankind. At the time, mediums were tremendously popular, and ghostly phenomena were very much in vogue, with the first memorable mediums being the Fox sisters of New York. Spiritism is an open, non-dogmatic belief system that seeks a deeper awareness of the relationship between our material world and the realm of spirit.

Initially skeptical, Kardec attended a number of seances, and became convinced there was more to the phenomena than mere trickery. He conducted a series of mediumistic experiments, and after receiving similar answers from a variety of mediums, began to compile his first book on Spiritism. The resulting text, called the Spirit's Book, is a compilation of questions on spiritual matters and the answers given by the spirits. This was followed by a number of other successful books, many of which were protested or burned by outraged Catholic clerics.

Spiritists believe in a universe populated by spirits, including those of humans. According to Spiritist beliefs, there are innumerable spirits, created by a God, a sole deity. The mission given to those spirits is to evolve from one state of spiritual existence to another, often through successive lifetimes.

Spiritism promotes a doctrine of continual spiritual evolution, from a 'sleeping' state to one of perfect awareness, through individual spiritual effort. Enlightened spirits (Spirit Guides) no longer need to incarnate on this plane but continue their spiritual evolution by 'guiding' those who still live on this earth. Spiritist doctrine divides the spirits into a hierarchy of increasing purity or enlightenment, with three spiritual orders subdivided into ten classes, from the base and impure, poltergeists, etc., to the highest orders of pure souls, such as archangels.

Famous Spiritists include Sherlock Holmes creator Arthur Conan Doyle and Carl Jung, the founder of modern day psychology. US President Abraham Lincoln was also rumored to have been a spiritualist.


**What is Espiritismo?**

Caribbean Spiritualism, is in many ways different from its European counterpart. Sometimes called Espiritismo or in very Africanized forms Espiritismo Cruzado, it inherited many influences from African and Amerindian cultures. Espiritismo has never had a single leader or epicenter of practice, and as such its practice varies greatly between individuals and groups. In all cases, Espiritismo has absorbed various practices from other religious and spiritual practices endemic to Latin America and the Caribbean, such as Roman Catholicism, Curanderismo (traditional, Latin American folk healing), Santeria, Palo and Vodou.

During Cuba's first war of independence (1868-1878), certain Cubans began to support the Espiritismo to the conservative style of Catholicism. Those who suffered the greatest in the war, particularly those living in the east, abandoned their belief system and turned to Espiritismo. As a result, Cuban Catholicism was criticized and discarded by many Cubans. The straightforward rituals and the possibility of a connection with the spirits of the deceased appealed to many Cubans during this period of hardships and social discontent.

Puerto Rican Espiritismo shares many similarities in its origins to Cuban Espiritismo. Educated Puerto Ricans used Espiritismo as a way of justification in their mission to free the country from the grasp of Spanish colonial hold. However, the religious movement encountered many setbacks in its early years in Puerto Rico. Those who were caught practicing it were punished by the government and ostracized by the Catholic Church. Allan Kardec's books made their way into the country and were received well by the educated class. The movement did not despite all the roadblocks, which had been set up to prevent its spread in the country. There were two divisions within Puerto Rican Espiritismo. The first division was a middle class movement, which utilized the Kardecian methods in an attempt to enhance the development of the country. The other division applied towards to lower classes in both the rural and urban settings. This division is known as "Indigenous Espiritismo" and is synonymous to Puerto Rico and is the most popular in the country. Puerto Rican White Table Espiritismo follows the same ritual practices as found in Cuba. The attempt to achieve spiritual communication through a medium was widely practiced all over the island.

## What is Espiritismo Cruzado?

Originally practiced by followers and descendants of Congo religion in Cuba, Espiritismo Cruzado is again a deeper amalgamation of Spiritist practice and Afro-Caribbean Religion. There are various spirits in Espiritismo Cruzado and all work under a specific Saint or Higher Spirit. There is for example Tata Francisco Siete Rayos who works under Shango/Siete Rayos/St.

Barbara's orders. Negra Francisca Siete Sayas on the other hand works under Madre de Agua/Yemaya/Virgen de Regla. This form of Spiritism also has a variety of other spirits and guides, such as the Native Indians of the Caribbean, the Tainos and Arawak. Those are referred to as Los Indios." The Gypsy Spirits are called Commision Cigana and spirits of Old Black Slaves are known as 'La Madama' if female, and 'El Congo' if male. Espiritismo Cruzado is essentially the Caribbean version of Brazilian Umbanda – and was, interestingly enough, established around the same time as Umbanda.

## The Boveda Espiritual

The practice of Espiritismo is centered around a special altar or shrine, called 'Boveda Espiritual'. This simple altar consists of a number of plain glasses (from one up to nine), a crucifix, incense, flowers mixed with some sweet basil, perfumes, books of prayers ( traditionally either 'La Coleccion', Allan Kardec's selected prayers, or the standard catholic prayer book) and of course candles. Some practitioners also include statues of Saints and Spirit Guides as well as pictures of diseased family members, bottles of rum, cigars and offerings of coffee, food, rosaries and icons. Some Bovedas even have small glass pyramids, jade Buddhas and a Monstrance (the Santisimo). This shrine functions as a place where people go to 'salute' the sprits and to commune with their guides on a daily basis. As each and every person has different spirit guides (who are, put together as a group, called Spiritual Court), it is only natural to see slight variations in individual Bovedas. What follows are instructions on how to set up a standard Boveda.

## Setting up the Boveda

Setting up a Boveda is fairly simple. Nonetheless, there are certain steps which should be followed. A small table, shelve, the top of a chest of drawers or a small cabinet are preferable places to set up a Boveda. It is best not to set up a Boveda in your bedroom or in a place that many people frequent. If it is not possible to dedicate a whole room to your Boveda, try and at least have it in a quiet corner or partitioned off. This being said, some Espiritistas also like to have their Boveda somewhat face the mail door of the house - yet again, hidden behind large plants!

To begin with, try and see your Boveda as a microcosm, a small universe on its own. It is a place where you go to communicate with your guides and ancestors and should be kept clean, straight and simple. The more items you add to your Boveda, the more complicated and sometimes confusing the interchange of communication can get. More is not always better, but simplicity and tidiness are sure keys to success!

Once you have chosen a place for your Boveda, clean the area spiritually. It is always best to clean your whole house or apartment thoroughly before setting up your Boveda for the first time. De-clutter your home, vacuum clean and air out your living space as much as you can. If you have dying plants, broken electrical items or empty bottles, jars and cans in your house, get rid of these also! After you have cleaned your house physically, open all doors and windows and fumigate with incense. Any Church incense or other cleansing and protecting mix will do the job! One word of advise though! Some practitioners prefer to use Native American Smudge sticks and bundles made of Sage, Lavender and Cedar. If you prefer to smudge your house with one of those bundles, please ensure to use either only Sage or a mix of Sage and Lavender. Cedar is for various reasons seen as a holy tree and it is taboo to be burned.

> *Tradition tells us, that it was the great Orisha Shango who created Orun, the home of the spirits. Cedar is sacred to Shango and we observe this taboo in honor of the creator of Orun!*

Once you have cleaned your house, wash the top of the table, the shelve, the top of a chest of drawers or the top of the small cabinet you have chosen for your Boveda with a solution of Florida Water, Holy Water and some other Spiritual Colognes of your choice. Let it dry and cover the space with a white cloth.

*White, within the African Traditional Religions, is the color of death. The body of the deceased is wrapped in white, certain things are covered in white to symbolize mourning and rest. What better color is there to start working wit the spirits of the dead then their own!?*

Now you will need 6 small and 1 large glass. These glasses should be new and fairly simple, without any decorations, engravings or markings of any kind. Before you can set those glasses on your Boveda, wash them thoroughly with a solution of white Rum, Florida Water and some dish-washing detergent. Rinse the glasses well and either let them dry naturally or polish them with a freshly washed towel. Once your glasses are completely dry, set them in a row and place one small mint leave in the bottom of each glass. Now light a cigar and blow smoke in each glass - the reason why we set our glasses in a row is to make it easier to blow smoke inside!

Open your tap and let the cold water run for a while, just to make sure that it is truly cold before you begin to fill your glasses. It is best to fill the largest glass first. Make sure that you fill it up as much as possible but carefully ensure that no water runs over the outside of the glass! Once all your glasses are filled with water, place the largest glass in the center of your soon-to-be Boveda and the six smaller glasses around it in a circle.

*The symbolism behind this is very simple! Some people say that the largest glass represents your Guardian Angel, who is your main spirit guide, and the 6 smaller glasses represent other spirits that walk with you. Another interpretation is that the largest glass represents again your mail spirit guide, who always walks with you, while the other 6 glasses represent the 6 directions - to your left and to your right, behind you and before you, above you and below you. As you set your Boveda up, you ask your Spiritual Court to protect you from all things that around you (left, right, behind, below), to guard your head and your thoughts (above you) and to make sure that your steps in life be firm and secure. Some Espiritistas use 9 glasses on their Boveda, but this is not a traditional way of working but comes from an intermix with the funeral customs of traditional Yoruba Religion with Espiritismo.*

Once you have your glasses arranged on your Boveda, add one or two white candles - to the left and to the right of your glasses. You can also place some flowers on your Boveda. A bunch of simple, white Carnations mixed with very few yellow and red ones works best. If you want, make some fresh coffee with brown sugar or poor a small glass of white rum and add this to your Boveda also. Some Espiritistas will also add pictures of their deceased family members or memorial prayer cards. But this is something you might only want to consider over time, as the communication between you and your guides gets stronger and deeper.

*Seven days after setting up your Boveda for the first time, you should take the water from the glasses and the petals of those flowers and prepare a spiritual bath for yourself! Offerings of food and drink are usually just dispersed in the trash bin outside your house.*

Now that everything is set, all that there is to do now is to 'open' your Boveda. Begin with the Basic Catholic Prayers at the beginning of this book and then move on to Prayers for Misa Espiritual from page 111.

You can - and should - also pray straight from your heart! Tell your guides that you dedicate this space to them, ask them to come and refresh themselves, refresh your life, guide you, guard you and communicate with you. An essential part of mediumship development is to spend time in front of your Boveda, communication with your guides.

Every seven days, refresh your Boveda by washing and refilling the glasses with cold water. Only when you set your Boveda for the first time should you add Mint leaves. But it is always good to blow the glasses with tobacco smoke. You can always use the water from your Boveda either for spiritual baths, or poor it outside your front door as a sign of protection and cleansing.

*Boveda Espiritual*

Every religion and spiritual tradition has its signs and salutes, and Espiritismo is no exception. Every time you approach your Boveda, extend the middle finger and index finger of both hands and tap three times on your Boveda. Even when you visit the house of an Espiritista and have a chance to salute their Boveda and pay homage to their guides, you can do the same.

When you approach the Boveda you should talk to your guides, stating with prayer and stating why you have come – to communicate! But also always listen and meditate. The spirits of the dead and your guides will start to speak to you, but you must clear your mind and listen. After a while you will be able to tell the difference between your thoughts and when spirit is speaking.

## Working the Boveda

There are also 3 different ways to 'work' a Boveda. It is most common to place six clear glasses of cool water in a circle around one bigger glass. This is done for protection.

Another way to set your Boveda is to place the glasses in a V-shape - the large glass furthers in the back and 3 glasses on either side, each a bit more to the sides. This is called 'sending your spirits to work' and is usually done when Novenas and special prayers are performed on the Boveda.

The third way of working a Boveda is to create a pyramid of glasses. This means that 3 glasses are placed in a row next to each other. On top of those are set 2 more glasses. On top of this 'pole' is set the 6th glass. The large glass is then placed in front of this construction. We say that this works for spiritual evolution and should be done especially when prayers for recently deceased family members are said (see page 159). Misa Spiritual, the central ritual of Espiritismo, is also performed in front of the Boveda.

# How to build bridges and starting communicating with your guides

1.) Create a routine! It is best to refresh your Boveda always on the same day and in circles of 7 days. If you have set your shrine up on a Sunday, always refresh it on a Sunday also.

2.) Ancestor shrines at home with pictures of the deceased, flowers, small offerings of coffee, cake, sweets, and white candles. Meditate, pray and talk to the ancestors. Express your desire to get to know them and to learn their wisdom

3.) Develop your mediumship! Start to listen to the advice of your guides, feel their presence, respond to their needs and desires and show your appreciation for their presence with flowers and small offerings of coffee, cake, sweets, candles

4.) Regularly visiting your Boveda. This goes beyond your weekly routine and can simply be a salute to your shrine when you come home in the evening, lighting a candle 'when you feel like it' or placing some coffee or food for your guides on the shrine.

5.) Take your needs, hopes, and wishes to your ancestors and let them help you to be successful and happy in your life - which is what your ancestors wanted you to be all along!

Much more information in the various types of Spirit Guides and ways of working with them is provided in the authors forthcoming publications. A series of 7 books, called *Working the Spirits*, will be available in 2008/2009.

## Mediumship Development

People always want to know how to develop their mediumistic abilities and in return expect an answer that will reveal the big secret as to how to be a 100% correct medium. But the answer is very simple, sometimes so simple that that it can be disappointing for some. There is no one thing that you can do, no one event that will make you a medium over night or in an instant. Mediumship Development is exactly what its name says – development over a period of time! Practice brings mastery! Regular attendance of your Boveda, time spent in prayer and meditation will open your senses to the messages of spirit. Meditation however does not necessarily mean to sit cross-legged on the floor, surrounded by crystals, soft music and burning incense. The Bible, in Psalm 1, verse 2 says about King David: *"But his delight is in the law of the LORD, and in His law he meditates day and night"*. To maintain communication with the world of spirit, to listen, communicate and 'tune in' to spirit is not something that should only be kept for a few hours every month, but needs to develop into 'delighting in it Day and Night'. What King David expresses is a deep love and devotion to understand the 'laws of god' and the mechanisms of the universe. The word meditation used in the original Hebrew, the language in which the Psalms were first written, is derived from a verb which can also mean *to ponder* or *to muse*, and is associated with fervor and burning coals. The above Psalm, when translated differently, can give us en enormous amount of insight into spirituality! The word used for law in the original Hebrew derives from the verb *yarah* which describes the event of an outpour of water or rain and can be associated with divine inspiration. I'm sure every Spiritist and every medium will here be reminded of the feeling of fervor and burning coals that comes with receiving inspiration from spirit!

The more time we spend contemplating on spiritual matters, communicating with spirit and 'fanning those burning coals', the deeper our mediumistic abilities will develop. To engage in prayer, withdraw from the world and 'daydream' about matters of spirit is an indispensable for the development of mediumistic abilities!

A number of prayers can be found from page 27. These include morning prayers, prayers to spirit and spirit guides and a variety of other devotions. Besides saluting the Boveda in the morning and evening and reciting those prayers on a regular basis and contemplating on spiritual matters, the following bath, taken once a week, can also increase mediumistic abilities:

## Spiritual Development Bath

A simple bath made from fresh Sage and cold water, taken once a week is used by various Espiritistas in Latin America. The bath is prepared in a large bowl, holding approximately 1 gallon of water. A good number of fresh Sage leaves are then added to the water. The leaves are mashed up by hand until the water takes on a dark green color. The bath is then covered with a white towel and placed either in front of or directly on the Boveda. A prayer is said to spirit and it is asked that the bath may increase mediumistic abilities and strengthen the link to the spirit world.

Once the candle is burned out, the cold bath is poured over the body, from the shoulders down.

## Misa Espiritual

The Misa Espiritual, or Spiritual Mass, is the central ritual of Espiritismo. The Misa is an Africanized version of the Kardecian practices described above. Often a Misa is called for to illuminate a spirit, spirit guide or a deceased relative, or because the spirits of the dead wish to relay a message to a person. Misa's are also performed on a regular basis to maintain an intimate contact with the spirits - they are essential elements in mediumship development! The Spiritual Mass also has the affect of helping the spirits of the spirit to attain a higher plane spiritually.

During a Misa everyone is equal. There is no hierarchy. If anyone sees, hears, or feels something they should respectfully follow the inspiration of spirit and speak. It is not uncommon for spirit to mount or possess one of the members, the spirit often cleansing and giving advice to the participants once the spirit's true nature and motives are determined. If the spirit is excessively disruptive or useless it is forced to depart using special prayers and actions which are designed for this purpose.

The way a Misa Spiritual is prepared and conducted can slightly very from practitioner to practitioner. Misa's held in the homes of initiated of Afro-Caribbean traditions normally require less preparation as these practitioners usually take precautions to protect their homes from unwanted spiritual influences at all times. If there are no other spiritual protection mechanisms in place or to add extra protection, the following preparations can be considered:

- Simple glassed with cold water and Camphor can be places in the 4 corners of the home

- A bowl of cold water and Anil plus a lit glass encased candle inside the bowl can be put by the front door

- The home should be fumigated with frankincense and myrrh or any other incense suitable for the occasion

It is always recommended to perform Misa in a clean and tidy environment. A good house cleaning should always precede any type of spiritual meeting. In particular, empty bottles and jars should be removed from the home and all rubbish bins should be emptied. Dirty dishes should be washed beforehand and all corners in the home should be clean and free.

It is not always necessary to perform a Misa in front of one's personal Boveda, but a table can be prepared as described above. No matter if the Misa is held in front of a personal Boveda or in front of a specially prepared table, a large bowl with cold water flower petals and as many different types of spiritual colognes, such as *Florida Water, Colonia 1800, Lotion Pompeia, Sandalwood Cologne* or any other spiritual cologne. Around the table are also placed a good number of chairs for all participants.

Some Espiritistas prefer to dress in white during Misa, or wear certain items of clothing associated with their personal spirit guides. Others follow a more lenient approach and wear what ever feels most comfortable. However, most Espiritistas will always cover their heads during Misa. It is also not uncommon to rub Cascarilla around one's belly button and on the back of the neck.

Once everyone has taken their place in the circle, the meeting is usually opened with prayer. Once the opening prayers have been said, the next step would be for every participant to cleanse themselves by stepping up to the table and wash with the flower and cologne water which has been placed in front of the table. Some Espiritistas prefer to use a wash cloth which is water and used by everyone to 'wash' over their auras. Others will simply wash their hands and auras in the mixture. Many people will then take their seats again and light cigars or pipes to invite the spirits.

But cleansing does not stop with this initial 'washing' at the beginning of the Misa. *Florida Water* or other colognes are usually passed around several times during the session for participants to cleanse themselves by washing over their heads and back of the neck with a few splashes of cologne.

After the initial cleansing, more prayers are said and spiritual songs are sung to invite the spirits to come and communicate with everyone present. These messages can come in the form of possession where one or more of the mediums become 'mounted' by spirit, or they can come as mediumistic messages which are relied without the phenomenon of possession but by inspiration. Sometimes spirits who visit the sitting by 'mounting' mediums will not only deliver messages but might also perform healing, cleansings or other spiritual exercises. This, however, does not always have to be the case.

Once the Misa has finished, the closing prayers are said and the bowl of water which has been placed in front of the table is emptied outside the house. The same goes for the bowl of water and Anil which has been placed by the door. If glasses with camphor have been placed in the corners of the home, then these can either be emptied immediately or left over night and the water then disposed off outside the house the following day.

It is also always recommended to either shower or wash with Florida Water before going to bed – Misas are usually held at night.

# PRAYERS

## Opening Prayer

We ask the Divine Spirit and all our spirit guides
and guardians be here tonight to watch over our work.
We ask that only good spirits be present and
that our spirit companions protect us from harm
and mischief from any troubled spirits who may
be attached, attracted or sent to this place.

## Basic Catholic Prayers

### Lord's Prayer

Our Father, Who art in heaven, hallowed be Thy name. Thy kingdom come,
Thy will be done, on earth as it is in heaven. Give us this day our daily bread;
and forgive us our trespasses as we forgive those who trespass against us; and
lead us not into temptation, but deliver us from evil. Amen.

### Act of Contrition

O my God, I am heartily sorry for having offended Thee, and I detest all my
sins, known and unknown, not only because I dread the loss of heaven and
dread the pains of hell, and not only because You art my Creator, my Redeemer
and my Sanctifier, but most of all because my sins have offended Thee, my God,
Who are all good in You and deserving of all my love. I firmly resolve, with the
help of Your grace, to confess my sins, to do penance and to amend my life.
Amen.

## Apostle's Creed

I believe in God, the Father Almighty, Creator of heaven and earth; and in Jesus Christ, His only Son, Our Lord; who was conceived by the Holy Ghost, born of the Virgin Mary, suffered under Pontius Pilate, was crucified, died, and was buried. He descended into Hell; the third day He arose again from the dead; He ascended into heaven, sitteth at the right hand of God, the Father Almighty; from thence He shall come to judge the living and the dead. I believe in the Holy Ghost, the Holy Catholic Church, the communion of saints, the forgiveness of sins, the resurrection of the body, and life everlasting. Amen.

## Hail Mary

Hail Mary, full of grace! The Lord is with thee. Blessed art You among women, and blessed is the fruit of your womb, Jesus. Holy Mary, Mother of God, pray for us sinners, now and at the hour of our death. Amen.

## Act of Faith

O my God, I firmly believe that You art one God in three Divine Persons, Father, Son and Holy Ghost; I believe that Your divine Son became man, and died for our sins, and that He will come to judge the living and the dead. I believe these and all the truths which the Holy Catholic Church teaches, because You hast revealed them, who canst neither deceive nor be deceived.

## Glory Be

Glory be to the Father, and to the Son, and to the Holy Ghost. As it was in the beginning, is now, and ever shall be, world without end. Amen.

# Morning Prayer

I *thank you for bringing me to the beginning of another day,*
*for guarding me through my sleep, to see the morning*
*and to look forward to the chores of another day.*

*I thank you most especially for not allowing me to offend my fellow man,*
*throughout yesterday, because you have ordained, that to serve god, according to*
*the divine laws, your children should be able to tell you, that they have succeeded*
*in resisting temptation, to do any wrongs against God,*
*the two hundred divinities, all the children of God*
*and the society in which they live.*

*Furthermore, in accordance with your Injunction, I have refrained from avenging*
*all wrongs done to me by my relations, friends and enemies alike.*

*I thank you for bringing me to the beginning of another day,*
*for guarding me through my sleep, to see the morning*
*and to look forward to the chores of another day.*

*I thank you most especially for not allowing me to offend my fellow man,*
*throughout yesterday, because you have ordained, that to serve god, according to*
*the divine laws, your children should be able to tell you, that they have succeeded*
*in resisting temptation, to do any wrongs against God, he two hundred*
*divinities, all the children of God and the society in which they live.*
*Furthermore, in accordance with your Injunction, I have refrained from avenging*
*all wrongs done to me by my relations, friends and enemies alike.*

*Help me also to neutralize all evil plans against me, just as you will neutralize any evil that I might be tempted to plan against my fellow being.*

*Because as you have proclaimed,*
*that is the universal secret to long life*
*and Enduring prosperity.*
*Protect me today as always from all dangers and evils in my abode,*
*place of work and in my interactions with others.*

*To believe in one GOD, all powerful,*
*sovereignty just and good;*
*In the soul, its immortality and its pre-existence*
*as the justification for the present life;*
*In the plurality of existences as the mechanism of moral*
*and intellectual improvement, reparation and atonement;*
*In the perfectibility of the most imperfect beings;*
*In the ever increasing happiness with perfection;*

*In the equitable reward of the good and the evil according to the principle: each*
*one will be recompensed according to his works;*

*In the impartial justice for all with no benefit,*
*privilege or exception to any creature;*

*In the dependence of life's trial duration on perfection;*

*In the human free-will, which enable us the choice*
*between the good and the evil;*

*In the continuity of the relations between the visible and invisible worlds;*

*In the fraternity that binds all past, present
and future beings both incarnate and discarnate;*

*To sustain that life on Earth is a provisional stage
of the spirit's life which is eternal;*

*To bravely accept life's tests, since the future
is more desirable than the present;*

*To practice charity by thoughts, words
and works in the broadest meaning of the term;*

*To strive for becoming each day better than the day before,
pulling out imperfection from the soul;*

*To submit all beliefs to the review of reason and free examination,
so as nothing accept blindly;*

*To respect all sincere creeds no matter how irrational they may seem;*

*Do not violate anyone's consciousness;
To recognize the unfolding of Nature's laws
which are God laws in the discoveries of Science.*

*Raise me above all misfortune.*

*Raise me above all misfortune that might come my way while on this earth.*
*Always bring me good fortune.*

*If death is near help us to avert it.*

*Avert death for all my children avert death for all those I include in my prayers.*
*May they not die young, may they not die in fire, may they not die in tragedy,*
*may they not die in shame, may they not die in water.*

*I beg you to look upon me with good eyes so the world will be favorable to me*
*and my children, may I be free from illness. Let me overcome my enemies*

*Let the world hear of me, know I am rich, know I have honor, know I have*
*prestige, know my children will be good.*

*Open the way to wealth for me, that the whole world will want the products of*
*my work, let death pass me by.*

*May I be known as a parent who produces good children,*
*who will stand behind me,*
*follow my guidance and bury me at the end of my life.*

*Remove all obstacles wherever I go in the world.*
*Protect me from death, disease, litigation, loss and hexing,*
*prevent harm from those who work hexes.*

*Let my name not be spoken with contempt, let my name be famous in the*
*world, let my lineage flourish in the world.*
*Let me live long and see my hair turn white.*

What follows is
**A collection of Selected Prayers**
by Alan Kardec.

## PRAYERS FOR ONESELF

### A Prayer in Order to ask that some defect within ourselves may be corrected

**Preface:** Our bad instincts result from the imperfections of our own Spirit, and not from our physical body. If this were not so then Man would be exempt from all responsibility. Our betterment depends on ourselves, because every person who has all their faculties has in everything the liberty to do or not to do. In order to do good the only thing lacking is will-power.

*Dear Lord, You gave me the necessary intelligence*

*so as to distinguish right from wrong.*

*Thus, on recognizing something to be wrong,*

*I am guilty in not struggling to resist the temptation.*

*Preserve me from pride which can prevent me*

*from perceiving my defects, and also from*

*the bad Spirits, who can incite me to continue in the wrong.*

*Amongst my 'imperfections I recognize*

*that I am especially inclined to...,*

*and if I am unable to resist,*

*it is because I have already acquired the habit*

*of giving in to it.*

Because You are just, You did not create us guilty
but with equal aptitude for good and for bad.
If I have preferred the bad road
it was because of my free-will.
But for the same reason that I had the liberty to do wrong,
I also have the liberty to do good
and therefore to change my pathway.

My actual defects are the remains of the imperfections
I brought from my past existences;
this is my original sin, from which I may liberate myself
through the action of my will
and with help from the good Spirits.

Accordingly, protect me kindly Spirits,
and above all my Guardian Angel, by giving me the strength
to resist evil suggestions and so be victorious in this battle.
These defects are the barrier which separate us from God,
and each defect surmounted is a step further along
the pathway of progress which will draw us nearer to Him.

O Lord, in Your infinite mercy,
You thought fit to concede me this present life so that
It would serve for my advancement.
Good Spirits, help me to take advantage of this opportunity
so that I may not lose it.
When it pleases God to remove me from it,
help me to leave it in a better condition than on entering.

# Prayer to Ask for Strength to resist Temptation

**Preface:** Every bad thought can have two origins: our own spiritual imperfection or the action of a harmful influence. In the last case we have the indication of a weakness which exposes us to these influences, and it is for this reason that our soul is imperfect. So that the one who foils cannot offer as an excuse the influence of a strange Spirit, seeing that this Spirit would not hove led them to wrongdoing if they were inaccessible to seduction.

When we have a bad thought, we can suppose that it was an evil Spirit which suggested the evil, leaving us complete liberty to accede or resist, just as if we were facing a living person. At the same time, we should make a mental picture of our Guardian Angel or protecting Spirit who from his side combats within us the bad influences and anxiously awaits the decision we are going to make. Our hesitation in acting upon the evil suggestions is due to the voice of our good Spirit, who makes himself heard through our conscience.

One recognizes a thought is bad when it draws away from charity which is the base of all true morality; or when it comes laden with pride, vanity and selfishness; or when its realization may cause harm to another person: in short, when we are induced by our thoughts to do to others what we would not like someone to do to us.

*All Powerful Lord,*

*do not let me succumb to the temptation to fall into error!*
*Benevolent Spirits who protect me,*
*turn this bad thought away from me*
*and give me the strength to resist this evil.*

*If I succumb, then I will deserve the expiation of my failing*

*in this same life and in the next,*

*because I have free will to make my choice.*

## Thanksgiving for Victory over a Temptation

**Preface:** Those who resist temptation owe this fact to the assistance given by the good Spirits, whose voice they listened to. So, you should thank God and your Guardian Angel for their help.

**M**y God, I thank You for having permitted me

*to be victorious in the battle which I sustained against evil.*

*Allow this victory to give me strength*

*to resist new temptations.*

*And you, my Guardian Angel, receive my thanks*

*for the assistance you gave.*

*Allow that my submission to your counsel makes me worthy*

*to receive your protection once again.*

# A Prayer to ask for advice

**Preface:** When we are unsure about something we have to do, before anything else, we should ask ourselves the following questions:

1st) Will what I am hesitating about cause harm to anyone?

2nd) Will it be useful to anyone?

3rd) If someone did this to me, would I be pleased?

If what we think of doing is of interest only to ourself, it is permissible to weigh the personal advantages or disadvantages which may arise. If it concerns others and if, in doing good for one person, it redounds in badness for another, it is also equally necessary to weigh the advantages and disadvantages before deciding whether to act or abstain.

Finally, even when dealing with the best of things it is necessary to consider the opportunity and the circumstances being offered, in as much as something that is good in itself con give bad results when put into the wrong hands, or if it is not directed with prudence and circumspection. Before putting it into effect it is best to consult our strength and the means of execution. In any case, we can always solicit the assistance of our Protecting Spirits, remembering this wise maxim: When in doubt, do nothing.

*In the name of God, the All Powerful One,*

*in my uncertainty, I call upon the good Spirits*

*who protect me to inspire me to make the best decisions.*

*Lead my thoughts always towards goodness*

*and protect me from the influences of those*

*who tempt me to stray.*

## Prayer in Afflictions of Life

**Preface:** We can ask God for earthly favors and He will concede them to us when they have a serious purpose. But seeing that we judge their utility from our own point of view and as immediate necessities, we do not always recognize the bad side of what we ask. God, who can see things in a better perspective than we can and only desires the best for us, may refuse what we ask for, just as a father would refuse his child what he knew would be prejudicial for him. If what we request is refused we should not be disappointed; on the contrary, we should think that to be deprived of our wish is a test or expiation, and that our recompense will be in proportion to the degree of resignation shown towards what we have to put up with.

God *Omnipotent, who sees all our miseries,*

*please deign to hear the supplication we direct to You*

*at this moment.*

*If my request is inconsiderate, forgive me.*

*If it is just and convenient,*

*according to the way You see things,*

*may the good Spirits who execute Your wishes,*

*come to my aid and help me to realize my request.*

*However it may be, Lord, let Your will be done!*

*If my request is not answered, it will be*

*because it is Your wish that I be tested,*

*and I submit without complaint.*

*Help me not to become*

*disseminated and that neither my faith*

*nor my resignation be shaken.*

# Thanksgiving for the Obtaining of a favor

**Preface:** We must not consider as blessed successes only those things which are of great importance. Frequently things that are apparently insignificant are those which most influence our destiny. Man easily forgets the goodness received, preferring to remember only afflictions. If we were to register day by day the many benefits we receive, without even having asked for them, we would be greatly surprised to perceive there are so very many that we have swept from our minds and would feel ashamed of our ingratitude.

On lifting up our soul to God each night, we should remember in our innermost self the many favors that He has granted us during the day and offer thanks for them. But most especially, at the moment we receive the effects of His goodness and protection, we should spontaneously bear witness to our gratitude. For this, it is enough that we direct a thought attributing the benefit to Him, without even interrupting our work.

Benefits from God are not limited to material things. We should also thank Him for the ideas and happy inspirations we receive. Whereas the selfish person attributes all of these things to his own personal merits, and the incredulous person to mere chance, the one who has faith renders thanks to God and the good Spirits. Long sentences are not necessary for this purpose. "Thank you, dear God, for the inspiration of that good thought", says more than a long prayer. The spontaneous impulse which makes us attribute to God what has happened to us, bears witness of an act of thanksgiving and of humility, which will earn us the sympathy of the good Spirits

**B**eloved Lord of infinite goodness,

*may Your name be blessed for the benefits conceded to me!*

*I would be unworthy if I were to attribute these happenings*

*to mere chance or to my own merit.*

*Good Spirits, you who execute God's wishes,*

*I thank you and most especially my Guardian Angel.*

*Turn away from me all idea of being proud*

*of what I have received and help me to make*

*use of it exclusively for good. Most of all, I thank ...*


## An Act of Submission and Resignation

**Preface:** When we are suffering an affliction, if we look for the cause, we will always find it in our own imprudence, thoughtlessness or in some past action. As con be seen, in these cases we have to attribute the suffering to ourselves. If the cause of an affliction cannot be found to stem in any way from our own actions, then we are dealing with a test in this life, or an atonement for an error committed in a previous one. In this case, by the nature of the expiation we can know the nature of the error, as we are always punished in the same manner as our sin.

In general, we can only see the evil that is present in our afflictions. We do not see the favorable consequences they may have later on. Goodness is frequently the outcome of a past evil, just as the cure far an illness results from the painful methods used to obtain it. In any case, we must submit to the will of God and courageously support the tribulations of life if we want them to count in our favor. These words of Christ could then be applied to us; "Blessed are those who suffer".

*Dear Lord, Your justice is supreme.*

*Therefore all suffering in this world*

*must have a just cause and be of use.*

*I accept the affliction which I am undergoing,*

*or which I have just suffered, as an atonement for my past errors and as a test for the future.*

*Good Spirits who protect me,*

*give me the necessary strength*

*to support this without complaining.*

*Help me to look at it as a providential warning,*

*may it enrich my experience, reduce my pride,*

*diminish my ambition, stupid vanity and selfishness.*

*In short, may it contribute to my progress!*

## Another Prayer

*Dear God,*

*I feel the need to ask You for the necessary strength*

*so as to support the test that You have sent me.*

*Allow my Spirit to be enlightened,*

*with the necessary understanding,*

*so that I can appreciate the full extent of a love*

*that afflicts because it desires to save.*

*I submit myself with resignation, dear Lord,*

*but I am so weak I fear I will succumb*

*if You do not uphold me.*

*Do not abandon me, Lord,*

*because without You I am nothing.*

## Another Prayer

I *lift up my eyes to You, Eternal Father,*
*and feel fortified. You are my strength, dear Lord,*
*do not abandon me!*
*I am crushed under the weight of my iniquities!*
*Help me! I recognize the weakness of my flesh!*
*Please, do not take Your eyes from me!*
*I am being devoured by an ardent thirst!*
*Make the spring of living water*
*burst forth to quench this thirst.*
*May my lips open only to sing Your praises*
*and not to complain about my afflictions!*
*I am weak, Lord, but Your love will sustain me.*

*Eternal Father, only You are great,*
*only You are the reason and the finality of my life!*
*Blessed be Your Name even if You make me suffer,*
*because You are the Lord and I*
*am an unfaithful servant I bow down before You*
*without complaint because only You are great,*
*only You are the aim of all our lives!*

## When in imminent danger

**Preface:** Through the dangers we run God reminds us of the frailty of our existence. He shows us that our lives are in His hands, and that being held by only a thread, it may break when we least expect it to happen. From this point of view privilege does not exist for anyone because the same alternatives are to be found for both great and small alike. If we look at the nature and the consequences of danger we will see in most cases that these consequences, if they are verified, will have been a punishment for a misdeed or for an unfulfilled duty.

*Almighty God, and you who are my Guardian Angel,*
*help me! If I must succumb, may God's Will be done.*
*If I am to be saved, may the rest of my life*
*be given to repay the evil I have*
*done, for which I am truly repentant.*

## Thanksgiving for having escaped a danger

**Preface:** By the danger we have been through, God shows us that from one moment to another we may be called to give account for the way in which we have utilized our life. This is to alert us to the fact that we should examine ourselves and mend our ways.

*Dear God! Dear Guardian Angel!*

*I thank you for the help I received*
*during the danger that threatened me.*
*May this danger be a warning to me*
*and enlighten me with respect to my errors*
*That have brought me this peril.*


*I understand, Lord, that my life is in Your hands*
*and that You may take it away when You see fit.*
*Inspire me then, through the good Spirits who protect me,*
*with the idea of how best to take advantage of the time*
*You grant to me in this world! Guardian Angel!*
*Uphold me in my decision to correct my faults*
*and to do all the good that is within my power to do,*
*so that I may arrive in the spiritual world*
*with fewer imperfections,*
*whenever it pleases God to call me!*


## Prayer At Bedtime

**Preface:** Sleep is for the purpose of resting the body; however, the Spirit needs no rest. While the physical senses are in a torpid state the soul partly frees itself from the body and enters into the enjoyment of its spiritual faculties. Sleep has been given to Man to enable him to repair both his organic and moral strengths. While the body recuperates the spent energies which have been used during the waking state, the Spirit fortifies itself amongst other

Spirits. From all he sees, all he perceives and from the advice he is given, he takes the ideas which occur to him afterwards, in the form of intuitions. This is the temporary return of the exile to his true world, a momentary liberty that is conceded to the prisoner.

But it sometimes happens, as it does in the case of perverse prisoners, that the Spirit does not always take advantage of these moments of liberty for the purpose of progress. If he has bad instincts, instead of seeking the company of the good Spirits, he seeks out those who are like himself and goes to those places where he may give vent to his tendencies.

So then, the person who is convinced of this fact will lift up their thoughts to God before they go to sleep. They will ask for advice from the good Spirits and all those whose memory is dear to them, so they may go to join them for the brief moments of liberty which are conceded to them. On awakening they will then feel fortified against evil and be mare courageous when facing adversities.

*Lord, for a few short instants my soul*

*will be together with other Spirits.*

*So I beg the good Spirits to come and give me counsel.*

*Guardian Angel, please help me to keep a lasting and*

*beneficial impression of this encounter on awakening!*

## On Sensing the Approach of Death

**Preface:** During our lifetime to have faith in the future, together with the elevation of our thoughts towards our future destiny helps in the process of rapid liberation of the Spirit because this weakens the links which tie it to the material body. So much so that quite frequently, even before the physical body has expired, the soul being impatient to be free, has already launched itself into the great immensity. The contrary being the case of the person who, having concentrated on all that is material, finds these ties more difficult to break and the separation more painful and difficult, to be followed by an awakening full of anxiety and perturbation in the after-life.

# Dear God,

*I believe in You and Your infinite kindness.*

*Therefore, I cannot believe that You have given Man*

*intelligence which allows him to gain knowledge of You*

*and an aspiration for the future,*

*so as to plunge him into nothingness.*

*I believe that my body is only*

*a perishable covering for my soul*

*and that when I cease to live,*

*I will awaken in the world of the Spirits.*


*Almighty God,*

*I feel that the ties which hold my soul to my body*

*are breaking*

*and that in a short while I will have to account*

*for the use to which I have put the life*

*that is now slipping away from me.*
*I know that I will experience the consequences*
*of the good and the bad that I have practiced.*
*There will be no possibility of illusions, no subterfuge.*
*My past will unfold before me*
*and I will be judged according to my works.*
*I will take nothing with me of earthly possessions*
*such as honors, riches, satisfactions of vanity or pride,*
*in short, everything which belongs to the body*
*will remain in this world.*
*Not even the most minute particle of these things*
*will accompany me, nor would they be of use to me*
*in the spiritual world.*
*I will take with me only what belongs to my soul,*
*that is to say, the good and bad qualities I possess,*
*which will be weighed on the balance of strict justice.*
*I know that the judgment will be even more severe*
*according to the number of times I refused*
*the opportunities that were given to me*
*to practice good due to the position I held on Earth.*

*Merciful God, may the depth of the sincerity*
*of my repentance enable it to reach out to You!*
*May You see fit to cast over me Your cloak of indulgence!*
*If You see fit to prolong my present existence,*
*may I utilize that time to make good,*
*as far as I am able, all the evil that I have done.*
*But if my hour has come,*

*I take with me the consoling thought that I*
*will be permitted to redeem myself by means of new tests,*
*so that one day I may deserve the happiness*
*of the elected ones.*

*If it is not given to me to enjoy*
*such perfect happiness immediately,*
*which is known only to those who are pre-eminently just,*
*I know nevertheless that I am not denied hope for ever.*
*Sooner or later I will reach my goal,*
*according to the amount of effort I put*
*into working towards that objective.*
*I know that good Spirits and my Guardian Angel*
*are near to receive me and that soon I shall see them,*
*just as they see me now.*
*I know too, that if I deserve it,*
*I will meet again all those I have loved here on Earth,*
*and that those I leave behind will later come to meet me.*
*One day we shall all be united for ever,*
*and until that time arrives*
*I will be able to come and visit them.*

*I know too, that I will re-encounter those I have offended,*
*may they forgive me for whatever they have*
*to reproach me for, such as my pride,*
*my hardness and my injustices,*
*so that their presence will not overwhelm me with shame!*

*I forgive all those who have either done or tried to do me harm,*
*I hold no rancor against them and beg You,*
*dear God, to forgive them.*

*Lord, give me strength to leave all the material pleasures*
*of this world without regret,*
*which are as nothing compared to the healthy*
*and pure delights of the world into which I am about to*
*enter, and where for those who are just,*
*there are no more torments, or miseries, and where only*
*the guilty are subject to suffering.*
*But even they always have the consolation of hope.*

*Good Spirits and you who are my Guardian Angel,*
*I implore you not to allow me to fail at*
*this supreme moment. If my faith should waver,*
*then cause the Divine Light to shine in my eyes,*
*so that it may be reanimated.*

# PRAYERS FOR OTHERS

## For Someone who is afflicted

**Preface:** If it is in the interest of the afflicted person to continue their test then any request we might make will not shorten it. But it would be a lack of charity to abandon this person, alleging that our prayer would not be heard. Apart from this, even if the test is not interrupted, they may obtain some degree of consolation that will lessen their suffering. What is really useful for someone who is supporting a test is courage and resignation, without which whatever they are going through will bring them no results, because without these attributes they will have to go through it all again. Therefore, it is with this objective in mind that we should direct our effort towards asking the good Spirits to help them, or by lifting their morale through counseling and encouragement, or even by helping them in a material way, if this is possible. In such cases prayer can have a decisive effect by directing a fluidic current towards them with the intention of fortifying their morale.

*Dear God of infinite goodness,*

*may it please You to soften the bitterness of the position in which X . . . finds himself, if this be according to Your will.*

*Good Spirits, in the name of God Almighty,*
*I beseech you to help in his afflictions.*
*If it is not in his interest to be spared this suffering,*
*make him understand that it is necessary for his progress.*
*Give him confidence in God and the future,*
*which will make him less bitter.*

*Also give him strength so that he does not give himself*

*up to despair, which will make him lose the fruits of*

*his suffering and make his future even more painful.*

*Conduct my thoughts to him so that these may*

*help him to maintain his courage.*

## An Act of Thanksgiving for a Benefit Received by Someone Else

**Preface:** Those who are not dominated by selfishness rejoice over the good that comes to their neighbor, even if they did not make a solicitation by means of prayer.

*L**ord, we thank You for the happiness*

*conceded to X...*

*Good Spirits, help him to see that this benefit is the consequence of God's goodness.*

*If the good received constitutes a test,*

*Please inspire him with thoughts about how to make*

*the best use of it and not become conceited, so it does*

*not redound to his detriment in the future.*

*You, the good Spirits who protect me and desire my*

*happiness, turn aside from me all sentiment*

*of jealousy or envy.*

# A Prayer for our Enemies and those who wish us Ill

**Preface:** Jesus said: Love your enemies. This maxim shows us all that is most sublime in Christian charity. But Jesus did not mean to say that we should have the same tenderness for an enemy as we have for a friend. By these words He teaches us to pardon offences, to pardon all evil done to us and to repay all evil with goodness. Apart from the worth that this conduct has in God's eyes, it also serves to show Man the nature of true superiority.

*Dear God, forgive ... . the evil he has done me
and still desires to do to me, as I wish You to forgive me;
I also ask him to forgive me for the offences
I have committed against him.
If this person has been put in my pathway as a test,
may Your Will be done.*

*Turn me away, dear Lord,
from any idea of cursing him and from all
other wicked sentiments against him.
Do not ever allow me to be happy at any misfortune
that may befall him, so as not to blemish my soul with thoughts which are not
worthy of a Christian.*

*Lord, may your mercy extend to him
and induce him to harbor better sentiments towards me!*

*Good Spirits, induce me to forget all evil*
*and remember only the good.*
*May neither hate,*
*rancor nor the desire to pay back evil*
*with evil enter my heart,*
*since sentiments of hate and vengeance*
*belong to bad Spirits,*
*be they incarnate or discarnate!*
*On the contrary, may I be prepared*
*to extend a friendly hand to him,*
*so repaying evil with goodness and help him if it is possible.*
*So as to test the sincerity of my words,*
*I beg You to give me an opportunity to be useful to*
*him, but above all, Lord,*
*preserve me from doing this out of pride*
*and ostentation, smothering him with humiliating generosity*
*which would only cause me to lose the fruits of my action,*
*since in that case, I would deserve these words of Christ:*
*You have already received your recompense.*

# Thanksgiving for Blessings received by our Enemies

**Preface:** To not desire evil towards your enemies is to be only partly charitable. True charity consists in wishing them well and in feeling happy about the good that comes to you.

*Dear God, in Your justice You saw fit to make X... happy,*
*and on his behalf I thank You,*
*despite the evil he has done to me and still tries to do.*
*If he seeks to use this benefit to humiliate me,*
*I accept this as a test of my capacity for charity.*

*Good Spirits who protect me,*
*do not let me become regretful because of this.*
*Turn away from me all jealousy and envy*
*which only degrades.*
*On the contrary, inspire me*
*with the generosity that elevates.*
*Humiliation comes from evil and not from goodness,*
*and we know that*
*sooner or later justice will be done to each one*
*according to their works.*

## Prayer for a Child that has just been born

**Preface:** Only after having passed through the tests offered by physical life can Spirits reach perfection. Those who are in an errant state await God's permission to return to an existence which can offer them progress, either by the expiation of their faults by means of the vicissitudes to which they will be subjected, or by the undertaking of a mission which will benefit humanity. Their advancement and future happiness will be in proportion to the manner in which they employ the time given to them on Earth. The duty of guiding their first steps and of leading them towards goodness is up to their parents, who will have to give an account to God for the degree of fulfillment they gave to this mandate. It was to help them that God made paternal and filial love a Law of Nature, a law which can never be transgressed with impunity.

(To be said by the parents)

# Dear Spirit,

*who has incarnated in the body of our child,*

*we bid you welcome.*

*We thank You, Almighty God,*

*for the blessing of this child.*

*We know that this is a trust You have deposited in us*

*and for which one day we will have to give an account.*

*If he (she) belongs to the new generation of Spirits*

*who are to inhabit the Earth,*

*we thank you Lord for this blessing!*

*If it is an imperfect Spirit, it is our duty to help him/her*

*progress towards goodness,*
*by means of counseling and good examples.*
*If he/she falls prey to evil through our fault,*
*we shall be responsible for this,*
*seeing that we shall have failed in our mission.*

*Lord, uphold us in this task and give us*
*the necessary strength and willpower so as to be able*
*to fulfill it to the best of our ability.*
*If this child has come to test our Spirits,*
*may Your will be done, Lord!*

*Good Spirits, who have watched over this birth*
*and will accompany this child during the course*
*of his/her new existence, do not abandon him/her.*
*Turn away from him/her all the evil*
*Spirits who will try to tempt him/her into badness.*
*Give this being strength to resist all their*
*suggestions and courage to suffer with patience*
*and resignation the tests which await here on Earth*

## Another Prayer

**D**ear God,

*You have entrusted me with the destiny*
*of one of Your Spirits,*

*therefore, Lord,*
*make me worthy of the task You have set me.*
*Grant me Your protection.*
*Illuminate my Intelligence*
*so that I may perceive right from the beginning*
*the tendencies of the one it is my duty*
*to prepare for ascension to Your peace.*

## Another Prayer

*God of infinite goodness,*
*since You have seen fit to permit the Spirit*
*of this child to come once again to undergo earthly trials,*
*destined to make it progress,*
*give it enlightenment enough*
*so that it may learn to know You,*
*love You and worship You.*
*Through Your omnipotence may this soul*
*regenerate itself from the source*
*of Your Divine Teachings.*
*That, under the protection of its Guardian Angel,*
*its intelligence may develop,*
*amplify and lead it to aspire to move closer to You.*
*May the knowledge of Spiritism be*
*A brilliant light which illuminates it throughout*
*the many choices of life.*

*And finally, may it learn to appreciate*
*the full extension of Your love,*
*which puts us to the test so that we may purify ourselves.*

*Lord, cast a paternal eye over this family to which You have entrusted this soul,*
*so that it may learn to understand the importance of its mission.*
*May the seeds of goodness within this child*
*germinate till such time as, by its own aspirations,*
*it elevates itself to You.*

*O Lord, may it please You to answer this humble prayer,*
*in the name of and by the worthiness of He who said:*
*"Let the little children come to me,*
*because the Kingdom of Heaven is*
*for those who resemble them."*

# For one who Agonizes

**Preface:** Agonizing is the prelude to the separation of the soul from the body. It can be said that at this moment the person h05 one foot on Earth and the other in the next world. Sometimes this phase is painful for those who are deeply attached to worldly things and who live more for the possessions of this world than those of the next one, or whose conscience is agitated by regrets and remorse. On the other hand, for those whose thoughts seek the Infinite and who are able to disengage themselves from matter, it is less difficult to break the links which tie them to the Earth and there is nothing of pain in these last moments. Only a thin thread links their physical body to their soul, while in the first case there are thick roots which hold them prisoner. In every case, prayer exercises a powerful action in the work of.

*Merciful and omnipotent God,*

*here is a soul who is about to leave its terrestrial covering*

*in order to return to the Spirit world,*

*which is the real homeland.*

*May it be given to them to make this*

*passing in peace and may You extend Your mercy to them.*


*Good Spirits, who have accompanied this person on Earth,*

*do not abandon them at this supreme moment.*

*Give them strength to support the last sufferings*

*which they need to pass through in this world,*

*for the good of their future advancement.*

*Inspire them to use any last glimmerings of*

*intelligence or any fleeting awareness they may have,*

*to the consecration of repentance for any faults.*

*Allow my thoughts to act in such a way so as to help them*

*achieve this separation with less difficulty,*

*and may this soul take the consolation*

*of hope with it at the moment of departure from this Earth.*

## For those who are sick

**Preface:** Illness belongs to the tests and vicissitudes of earthly life. It is inherent in the grossness of our material nature and in the inferiority of the world we inhabit. Passions and excesses of all kinds create unhealthy conditions in our organism, which are sometimes transmitted by heredity. In worlds that are more advanced in both physical and moral aspects, the human organism, being more purified and less material, is no longer subject to the same infirmities and the body is not secretly undermined by the corrosives of passions. In this manner we must resign ourselves to the consequences of the ambient in which our inferiority places us, until we deserve to pass on to a better one. However, while we are waiting this does not prevent us from doing whatever we can to improve our present situation. But if despite our best efforts we do not manage this, then Spiritism teaches us to support our passing miseries with resignation. If God had not wished that in certain cases bodily sufferings be dissipated and softened, He would not have put the possibility of cure within our reach. His solicitude in this respect, being in conformity with the instinct of self-preservation, indicates that it is our duty to seek these means and apply them.

Apart from ordinary medication elaborated by Science, Spiritual Healing in its various forms allows us to know the power of fluidic action, and Spiritism reveals another powerful force in the mediumship of healing and the influence of prayer.

# Lord,

*You are all justice.*
*The illness You saw fit to send me must be deserved,*
*because You never impose suffering without just cause.*
*Therefore I entrust my cure to Your infinite mercy.*
*If it pleases You to restore my health,*
*may Your Name be blessed!*
*If on the contrary it is necessary*
*For me to suffer more,*
*may You be blessed just the same.*
*I submit without complaint to Your wise purpose,*
*since what You do can only be for the good*
*of Your creatures.*

*Dear God, let this infirmity be a timely warning to me,*
*which will cause me to meditate upon myself.*
*I accept it as an expiation for my past*
*and as a test of my faith*
*and submission to your blessed will*

## For the sick person

**D**ear God,

*Your designs are impenetrable
and in Your wisdom You have sent
this affliction to X... I implore You, Lord,
to cast a glance of compassion over his sufferings
and if You see fit, to terminate them.*

*Good Spirits,
you who are ministers of the Almighty,
I beseech you to second my request
To alleviate his sufferings,
direct my thought so that a balsam
may be poured over his body
and consolation poured into his soul.
Inspire him with patience and submission to God's Will.
Give him enough strength to support
The pain with Christian resignation,
so that the fruits of this test may not be lost.*

## A Prayer To be said by the Healer

**D**ear God,

*if it pleases You to use me as an instrument,*
*although I am unworthy,*
*may I cure this infirmity if You so desire,*
*because I have faith in You.*
*But I know I can do nothing alone.*
*Permit the good Spirits*
*to concentrate their beneficial fluids in me,*
*so that I may transmit them to the sick person*
*and free me from all thought of pride and selfishness,*
*which might alter their pureness.*

## Prayers for those who are obsessed

**Preface:** Obsession is the persistent action which an inferior or bad Spirit exercises over an individual. It may present many varied characteristics, from a simple moral influence with no perceptible exterior signs, to a complete organic and mental perturbation. It may obstruct all mediumship faculties. In automatic-writing this may be shown by the insistence of one Spirit in communicating, to the exclusion of all other Spirits.

Bad Spirits encircle the Earth, due to the moral inferiority of its inhabitants. Their malevolent action forms part of the afflictions which face humanity. Obsessions, just as much as infirmities and all life's tribulations, must be considered as tests and atonements and accepted as such.

In the same manner that sicknesses are the result of our physical imperfections, which make the body accessible to pernicious exterior influences, obsession is always the result of moral imperfections, which allow the access of a bad Spirit. Physical causes pit themselves against physical forces; a moral cause must be opposed by a moral force. In order to prevent infirmities we fortify our bodies; to exempt ourselves from obsession it is necessary to fortify the soul, which means that the obsessed person must work for their own betterment, which is frequently sufficient to relieve them of the obsession without resorting to help from others. When an obsession degenerates into subjugation and possession, then the help of other people becomes indispensable, because not infrequently the patient loses their will-power and their free-will.

Obsession almost always manifest the vengeance that a Spirit desires, which is frequently rooted in the relationship they had with this person in a previous life (See chapter 10, item 6 and chapter 12, items 5 & 6 of *THE GOSPEL ACCORDING TO SPIRITISM*).

In the case of a grave obsession, the person being obsessed is enveloped and impregnated by pernicious substances, so neutralizing the action of healthy fluids and repelling them. It is very important to free the person from these negative vaporous fluids. However, a bad fluid cannot be eliminated by other bad fluids. By a similar action to that exercised by a healer in the case of illness, it is necessary to expel the bad substances with the help of better ones, which in a certain way produces the effect of a reaction. This may be called a mechanical action, but it is not sufficient alone. It is also necessary and most important, to act upon this intelligent being by speaking with authority, which can only be achieved through moral superiority. The greater this is, the greater will be the authority.

This is not all however. In order to guarantee liberation from the obsessor it is also necessary to induce the perverse Spirit to renounce their bad designs, to awaken repentance in them and a desire to do good. This can be done through the means of skillfully directed instruction, given during special private meetings for this purpose, with the objective of offering moral education to this Spirit. Then it may be possible to have the double satisfaction of liberating an incarnate Spirit and converting a discarnate one at the same time.

This task is made easier when the obsessed person, understanding their situation, joins in with the prayers and adds their cooperation in the form of a desire to recuperate. The same does not happen when, being seduced by the obsessing Spirit, the person remains deluded as to the qualities of the entity who dominates them, even taking pleasure in the errors this Spirit induces them to commit. In this case, instead of helping, he repels all assistance offered. This is what happens in cases of fascination, which are infinitely more rebellious to treatment than even the most violent case of subjugation (See *THE MEDIUMS' BOOK*, (1) chapter 23). In all cases of obsession, prayer is the most powerful means of help in the action against an obsessing Spirit.

## A Prayer To be said by the person being obsessed

**D**ear God,

*permit the good Spirits to liberate me*
*from the malefic Spirit which has linked itself to me.*
*If this Spirit is seeking vengeance*
*as a consequence of wrongs I might have practiced*
*against him in other existences,*
*then You have permitted this,*
*Lord, and I suffer for my own faults.*
*May my repentance make me worthy*
*of Your pardon and of my liberation!*

*But whatever the motive,*
*I beseech Your mercy for he who persecutes me.*
*Lord; help him to find the pathway to progress,*
*which will turn him away from the practice of evil.*
*May I, on my part, repay evil with goodness,*
*so inducing him to better sentiments.*

*But dear God, I also know that it is my own*
*imperfections which make me accessible*
*to the influences of imperfect Spirits.*
*Give me the necessary light*
*so I may recognize these imperfections*
*and above all, remove the pride in me*
*which makes me blind to my own defects.*

*How great must be my unworthiness*
*to allow a malefic being to dominate me!*
*Dear God, may this blow to my vanity*
*be a lesson for the future.*
*May it fortify the resolution I have made*
*to cleanse myself by means of the practice*
*of goodness, charity and humility,*
*so that as from now I may put up a barrier*
*against all bad influences.*
*Lord, give me strength to support*
*this test with patience and resignation.*
*I understand that,*
*just as with all other tests,*

*it will aid my progress if I do not spoil*

*the fruits with my complaining,*

*because it offers me an opportunity to demonstrate*

*my submission and to practice charity*

*towards an unhappy brother*

*by forgiving him the evil he has done me.*

## A Prayer For the one who is obsessed

**A**lmighty God,

*may it please You to give me*

*the power to liberate X...*

*from the influence of the Spirit that is obsessing him.*

*If it be in Your designs to put an end to this test,*

*concede me the grace of speaking to this Spirit*

*with the necessary authority.*

*I ask all good Spirits who help me,*

*and you, his Guardian Angel,*

*to give me your assistance,*

*help me to free this sufferer*

*from the impure fluids which envelop him.*

*In the name of Almighty God,*

*I urge the malefic Spirit which torments this person to retire!*

## A Prayer For the obsessing Spirit

Lord of infinite goodness,
I implore Your mercy for the Spirit who is obsessing X...
Help him to see the Divine Light
so that he may recognize
the falsity of the path he follows.
Good Spirits, help me make him understand
that he has everything to lose by the practice of evil,
and everything to gain by the practice of good.

To the spirit who is tormenting X...,
I beg you to listen to me
since I speak to you in the name of God!
If you would but reflect,
you would understand that evil can never outdo goodness
and that it is not possible to be stronger
than God and the good Spirits.
It is possible for them to protect X.... from your attacks,
if this has not been done already
it is because he had to go through this test.
But when this test reaches its end,
then all action against him will be blocked.
The evil that you have done, instead of causing harm,
will have contributed towards his progress and happiness.
In this manner, your wickedness will be a total loss
for you and will only rebound upon yourself.

*God, Who is all powerful,*

*and the Superior Spirits who are His delegates,*

*being more powerful than you,*

*are capable of putting an end to this obsession*

*whenever they wish, and your tenacity will fall*

*before this supreme authority.*

*But because He is good,*

*God wants to leave you the merit*

*for having ceased of your own will.*

*It is a respite that is being offered to you,*

*and if you do not take advantage of it you*

*will suffer deplorable consequences.*

*Great punishment and cruel*

*suffering will await You will be forced to plead for mercy*

*and for the prayers of your victim,*

*who has already forgiven you and prays for you,*

*which constitutes a great merit in the eyes of God*

*and hastens their liberation.*

*So reflect while there is still time,*

*seeing that God's justice will fall upon you*

*as it does on all rebellious Spirits.*

*Consider that the evil you do now necessarily has a limit,*

*whereas, if you persist in being obstinate,*

*you will only increase the extension of your own sufferings.*

*When you were upon Earth,*

*did you never consider it stupid*

*to sacrifice a great goodness*

*for a small momentary satisfaction?*

---

*It is the same now you are a Spirit.*

*What will you gain by what you are doing?*

*The misguided pleasure of tormenting someone,*

*which does not stop you being*

*wretched even if you do not admit it,*

*only leaves you even more unhappy.*

*On the other hand, see what you are missing!*

*Look at the good Spirits around you*

*and tell me if their lot is not preferable to yours.*

*The happiness they enjoy*

*can also be yours whenever you like.*

*What do you have to do for this?*

*Beseech God, and instead of doing evil, do good.*

*I know that you cannot transform yourself immediately,*

*but God does not demand the impossible;*

*He only asks for good-will.*

*Try, and we will help you.*

*Make an effort so that very soon we may offer up*

*in your name the prayer for those who are repentant,*

*and no longer rank you amongst the bad Spirits,*

*while we await the moment when we can count you*

*among the good Spirits.*

# PRAYERS FOR THOSE NO LONGER ON EARTH

## Prayer for someone who has just died

Preface: Prayers for those who have just left the Earth ore not for the exclusive purpose of showing our sympathy. They also have the effect of helping to release them from their Earthly ties, and in this manner shorten the period of perturbation which always follows the separation, so allowing a more peaceful awakening on the other side. Nevertheless, in this case, as in all other circumstances, the efficacy depends on the sincerity of the thought and not on the quantity of words offered with more or less solemnity in which very frequently the heart does not participate.

Prayers which truly come from the heart encounter a resonance in the Spirit to whom they are directed, whose ideas are still in a state of confusion; as if they were friendly voices come to awaken them from sleep.

*A*lmighty God

*may Your mercy be shown to the soul of X . . .*
*whom You have just called back from Earth.*
*We beg and implore that the trials*
*suffered here may be counted in their favor*
*and that our prayers may soften and shorten*
*the penalties still to be suffered in the Spirit form!*

*Good Spirits who came to fetch this soul,*
*and most especially their Guardian Angel,*

*help them to free themselves from matter.*
*Give them light and a consciousness*
*of themselves so that they may quickly leave*
*the state of perturbation,*
*inherent in the passing from the body*
*back to the spiritual life.*
*Inspire in their Spirit a repentance for all errors*
*and faults committed and a desire*
*to obtain permission to remedy them,*
*so as to quicken their advancement in the direction*
*of the life of those who are eternally blessed.*


*And you, X...*
*who have just entered into the World of the Spirits,*
*we wish to say that despite this fact,*
*you are still with us,*
*you hear and see us, since you have merely*
*left the perishable physical body,*
*which will quickly be reduced to dust.*
*You have left the gross envelope which*
*is subject to vicissitudes and death,*
*now retaining only your etheric body which is imperishable*
*and inaccessible to material suffering.*
*If you no longer live through a physical body,*
*you live instead through your Spirit,*
*and the spiritual life is free from those*
*miseries which afflict humanity.*
*You no longer have over your eyes the veil*

*which hides the splendors of*
*the future existence from us.*
*Now you may contemplate new marvels,*
*while we remain bathed in darkness.*
*You may travel through space*
*and visit the worlds in all liberty,*
*while we still painfully drag ourselves about here on Earth,*
*prisoner in our material bodies, which are like heavy armor.*

*The infinite horizons stretch themselves before you,*
*and on seeing their grandeur you will*
*understand the vanity of terrestrial desires,*
*of worldly aspirations and the futility of the so-called*
*joys to which Man delivers himself.*
*For Man, death is nothing more than*
*a separation from matter, lasting but a few instants.*

*From this place of exile in which we continue*
*to live according to the Will of God,*
*and with the duties we still have to fulfill in this world,*
*we will continue to follow you in thought till the moment*
*when it is permitted for us to join you once again,*
*just as now you are reunited with those who preceded you.*
*We cannot go to where you are, but you may come here.*
*So come then to those who love you*
*and whom you love; help them in the trials of life,*
*watch over those who are dear to you,*
*protect them as much as you are able,*

*lessen the bitterness of absence*
*by suggesting to them the thought*
*that now you are happier and that one day,*
*for certain, you will again be reunited in a better world.*
*In the place you are now,*
*you must extinguish all earthly resentments.*
*You must hold yourself inaccessible to them now,*
*for the sake of your future happiness!*
*Therefore forgive all those*
*who may have incurred debts towards you,*
*just as those against whom mistakes were*
*committed now forgive you.*

## Another Prayer

*All Powerful Lord,*
*may Your mercy extend over all those*
*brothers and sisters who have just left the Earth!*
*May Your light shine upon them!*
*Remove them from darkness!*
*Open their eyes and ears!*
*May the Good Spirits surround them*
*and let them hear Your words of hope and peace!*
*Lord, even though we are not worthy,*
*we beg and implore Your merciful indulgence for this*
*brother (or sister) who has recently been recalled from exile.*

*Make their return that of the prodigal son.*
*Forget, O Lord, the faults they may have committed*
*and remember only the good they have done.*
*Your justice is immutable, as we know,*
*but Your love is immense.*
*We beseech You therefore,*
*to mitigate Your justice from the fountain of kindness*
*which emanates from You!*


*You who have just left the Earth,*
*may the light shine brightly before your eyes, my brother!*
*May the good Spirits come to be near you,*
*to surround you and help you to break your earthly chains!*
*Now you can understand and see the grandeur of God:*
*so submit yourself without complaint to His justice, however,*
*never despair of His mercy.*


*Dear brother! (or sister)*
*May a profound examination of your past*
*open the doors of the future,*
*by making you understand the*
*errors you have left behind,*
*as well as the work that awaits,*
*so you may remedy them!*
*May God forgive you and may the good Spirits*
*uphold and animate you!*
*Your brothers and sisters on Earth*
*will pray for you, and ask that you pray for them.*

# Those for whom we have affection

**Preface**: How terrible is the idea of nothingness! How deserving of pity are those who think that the voice of one who weeps is lost in a vacuum, without encountering the least sign of response! A pure and saintly affection has never been known by those who think everything dies with the body. They believe that the genius who enlightened their world with vast intelligence, is a mere combination of matter which, as a flame, is extinguished for ever; that of a dearly loved person such as a father, mother or adored child, nothing remains but a handful of dust which time will inevitably disperse.

How can anyone who has a heart remain indifferent to this idea? Why are they not frozen with terror at the thought of absolute annihilation and do not even show a wish that this be not so? If till now reason has been insufficient for them to have been able to dissipate their doubts, behold, Spiritism has come to dispel all uncertainty as to the future, by means of the material proof of survival of the soul and the existence of beings in the beyond that it gives! This is happening to such an extent, that on all sides these proofs are being received with joy. Confidence is reborn, because Man henceforth knows that terrestrial existence is only a brief passage leading to a better life, that work done in this world is not lost and that really pure affections are not shattered beyond hope.

# O *Lord,*

*may You see fit to favorably receive*

*this prayer in the name of X...*

*Help them*

*perceive the divine lights*

*that will make their pathway to eternal happiness easier.*

*Permit the good Spirits*
*to take them my words and thoughts.*
*You who were so dear to me in this world,*
*listen to my voice which calls to offer anew*
*my pledge of affection.*
*God allowed you to be liberated before me*
*and I cannot complain about this*
*without being selfish, because this would be equal*
*to a wish that you be still subject*
*to the sufferings of life.*
*So wait with resignation for the moment*
*of our reunion in this happier world,*
*where you have arrived before me.*
*I know that this separation is only temporary,*
*and that however long it may appear to be,*
*its duration is nothing compared to the blessed*
*eternity which God has promised to His chosen ones.*
*May His goodness preserve me from doing*
*whatever it might be that could delay this longed for*
*moment, so that I may be saved from the pain*
*of not encountering you*

*when I leave my earthly captivity.*
*Oh, how sweet and consoling*
*is the certainty that there is nothing between us*
*but a material veil which hides you from my sight!*
*That you can even be here at my side,*
*hear me speak as of old,*

*or perhaps even better than then;*

*to know that you do not forget me as I do not forget you;*

*that our thoughts are constantly intermingling and that your thoughts accompany me and uphold me.*

*May the peace of the Lord be with you.*

## For Suffering Spirits who ask for Prayers

**Preface:** So as to appreciate the relief that prayer gives to suffering Spirits, it is necessary to remember by what manner this is achieved, as has been previously explained Those who are convinced of this fact will be able to pray with greater fervor, because of the certainty that they do not do so in vain.

G*od of clemency and mercy,*

*may Your goodness extend to all the Spirits*

*we have recommended to You in our prayers,*

*especially the Spirit of X …*

*Good Spirits, whose only occupation is to do good,*

*intercede together with me for their relief.*

*Make a ray of hope shine before their eyes*

*and enlighten them as to the imperfections which*

*maintain them distant from the homes of the blessed.*

*Open their hearts to repentance*

*and the desire to cleanse themselves,*

*so they may accelerate their advancement*
*Make them understand it is by*
*their own efforts that they may shorten*
*the duration of their trials.*
*May God, in all His goodness,*
*give them the necessary strength*
*to persevere with their good resolutions!*

*May these words, infused with benevolence,*
*soften their trials, so showing them that there*
*are on Earth those who sympathize*
*and wish them happiness.*

## Another Prayer

**W***e ask, Lord,*
*that You shower the blessings of Your love*
*and mercy on all who suffer,*
*be they wandering Spirits or incarnates.*
*Have pity for their weaknesses.*
*You made us fallible,*
*But gave us the capacity to resist evil and conquer it.*
*May Your mercy extend to all those who*
*are not able to resist their evil tendencies*
*and still continue to drag themselves*

*along evil pathways.*
*May the good Spirits surround them,*
*may Your light shine in their eyes,*
*and so attracted by the life-giving*
*warmth of this light,*
*may they come to prostrate themselves at Your feet,*
*humbly, repentant and submissive.*

*Merciful Father,*
*we also ask for those of our brothers and sisters*
*who have not had the strength*
*to resist their earthly trials.*

*Lord, You gave us a burden to carry,*
*to be laid only at Your feet.*
*However, our weaknesses are great*
*and our courage fails us sometimes during*
*the course of the journey.*
*Have pity on these indolent servants*
*who have abandoned the work before time.*
*May Your justice spare them*
*and allow the good Spirits to take them some relief,*
*consolation and hope for the future.*
*The prospect of pardon strengthens the soul,*
*Lord, show this pardon to those*
*Guilty ones who have given themselves up to despair,*
*so that upheld by hope they may absorb*
*enough strength from the actual immensity*

*of their failings and sufferings,*

*so they may redeem the past*

*and prepare themselves for the conquest of the future.*

## Prayer for an Enemy who has died

**Preface:** Charity towards our enemies should accompany them into the Beyond. We need to understand that the evil they did was a test for us, which can be useful to our state of advancement, if we know how to take advantage of it. It can be even more beneficial to us than purely material afflictions, by the fact of our being allowed to join together courage, resignation, charity and the forgetting of.

# L*ord,*

*it pleased You to call the soul of X...*

*before You called me. I forgive him the evil*

*he did and the bad intentions nurtured towards me.*

*Maybe he is regretting this now that he no longer*

*feeds off the illusions of this world.*

*Dear God, may Your mercy descend upon him*

*and turn away from me any idea I might*

*have of rejoicing at his death.*

*If I am in debt towards him for any reason,*

*may he forgive me,*

*as I forget those misdemeanors committed against me.*

# For a Criminal

**Preface:** If the efficiency of prayer was proportionate to its length, then the longest ones would be reserved for the most guilty, because they are in more need than those who have lived saintly lives. To refuse prayer to criminals is to Lack charity towards them and to be unaware of the mercy of God. To believe they would be useless because a man has committed this or that grove crime would be to prejudge the Almighty's justice.

Lord God of Mercy,

*do not repudiate this criminal*

*who has just left this Earth!*

*Man's justice has condemned him,*

*but this does not exempt him from Your justice,*

*if his heart has not been touched by remorse.*

*Take away the blind-fold that hides the gravity of his faults!*

*His repentance may deserve*

*Your kindly treatment*

*and soften the sufferings of his soul.*

*Our prayers can also help*

*and the intercession of the good Spirits*

*may offer him hope and consolation.*

*Inspire in him the wish to*

*make amends for his actions in another existence*

*and give him strength so as not to succumb*

*in the new battles which he will undertake!*

*Lord, have pity on him!*

## Prayer for a Suicide

**Preface:** Man never has the right to dispose of his life, since it is only given to God to retrieve him from captivity on Earth, when He judges opportune. Nevertheless, Divine justice may soften the rigors in accordance with the circumstances, reserving however all severity towards he who wished to evade the trials of life. The suicide is like a prisoner who escapes from prison before he has served his sentence, and who when recaptured is treated with greater severity. The same happens with a suicide who imagines he is escaping from the miseries of the moment, only to plunge into even greater misfortunes.

*We know, Lord, the destiny that awaits*

*those who violate Your law,*

*by voluntarily abbreviating their days.*

*But we also know that Your mercy is infinite.*

*So please condescend to*

*extend this mercy to the soul of X...*

*May our prayers and Your commiseration lessen*

*the harshness of the sufferings they are experiencing*

*for not having had the courage*

*to await the end of their trials.*


*Good Spirits, whose mission it is to help those*

*who are wretched, take this Spirit under your protection,*

*inspire him to regret the error committed.*

*May your assistance give him strength to*

*support with greater resignation*

*the new trials through which he will have*

*to pass in order to make reparation.*

*Turn aside from him the evil Spirits*

*who are capable of once again impelling him*

*towards that same act and so prolonging his sufferings*

*by making him lose the fruits of future expiations.*

*We also direct ourselves to you,*

*whose unhappiness is the motive for our prayers,*

*to offer a wish that our commiseration*

*may diminish the bitterness and help to create*

*within you the hope for a better future.*

*This future lies in your hands,*

*believe in the goodness of God,*

*whose bosom opens*

*to accept all repentance*

*and only remains closed to hardened hearts.*

## For Repentant Spirits

**Preface:** It would be unjust to include in our category of evil Spirits the suffering and repentant ones who ask for prayers. They may have been bad; nevertheless, they no longer are, ever since they recognized the error of their ways and deplore them; they are only unhappy. Some of them have even begun to enjoy relative happiness.

**G**od of Mercy,

who accepts the sincere repentance of the sinner,

be they incarnate or discarnate,

here is a Spirit who has taken pleasure in evil,

who recognizes his errors and is entering

into the good pathway.

Condescend, Lord, to receive him

like the prodigal son and forgive him.

Good Spirits, whose voices he did not pay attention

to but now wishes to hear,

permit him to glimpse the happiness

of the elected ones of the Lord,

so that he may persist in his desire

to purify himself in order to be able to reach them.

Uphold him in all his good intentions and give him

the necessary strength to resist his bad instincts.

To the repentant Spirit of X...,

we offer our congratulations for the inner changes

*you have made and we thank the good Spirits*
*who have helped you to do this.*
*If you previously took pleasure in evil,*
*it was because you did not understand how sweet*
*is the enjoyment of doing good,*
*and also because you felt too lowly to be*
*able to manage to do it.*
*But, from the moment you placed your first step*
*on the path of goodness a new light shone in your eyes.*
*Then you began to enjoy an unknown happiness*
*and hope entered your heart.*
*This is because eGod always hears the prayer*
*of a sinner who repents;*
*He never repels anyone who seeks Him.*
*So to be once again completely within God's grace,*
*you must apply yourself from now on*
*to not only never again committing evil but to doing good,*
*and above all else to repair the evil that you have done.*
*Then you will satisfy God's justice,*
*each good action you practice will wash away all past errors.*
*The first step has been taken,*
*so now as you continue to advance by this path*
*it will become easier and more agreeable.*
*Persevere then, and one day you will have*
*the glory of being counted*
*amongst the good Spirits and those who are blessed.*

# For Hardened Spirits

**Preface:** The bad Spirits are those who hove not yet been touched by repentance, who delight in evil and who feel no regrets for this. They are insensitive to reprimands, repel prayer and frequently blaspheme in God's name. They are those hardened Spirits, who after death seek vengeance upon men for the suffering they had endured and pursue with hate all who practiced evil against them during their existence, by either obsessing them or by exercising all kinds of disastrous influences over them.

There are two distinct categories of perverse Spirits: those who are plainly evil and those who are hypocrites. It is infinitely easier to bring the first ones back to goodness than the last ones. The first, more often than not, have brutal and coarse natures, just as is seen in men; they practice evil more from instinct than from calculation and do not seek to appear better than they are. However, there is in them a latent germ that needs to open up, which is usually achieved by means of perseverance; firm benevolence, counseling, reasoning and prayer. It h05 been noticed that in automatic-writing these Spirits have difficulty in writing the name of God, which is a sign of an instinctive fear, an intimate voice of conscience which tells them they are unworthy. It is at this point that they ore ready to convert themselves and we can hove high hopes for them; we only need to find the vulnerable point in their hearts.

Hypocritical Spirits are almost always very intelligent. But they do not have a grain of sensitivity in their hearts; nothing touches them. They simulate all the good sentiments so as to gain confidences and are happy when they encounter those who are foolish enough to accept them as good Spirits, because then they can control them as they like. The name of God, far from inspiring the least tremor of fear, serves them as a mask to cover their vileness. In both the invisible and visible worlds, the hypocrites are the most dangerous of beings because they act in the shadows, without anyone suspecting; they have only apparent faith, never real faith.

**L**ord,

*may it please You to cast a kindly glance*
*over the imperfect Spirits who find themselves*
*in the obscurity of ignorance and so do not know You,*
*especially the Spirit of X ...*


*Good Spirits, help us to make them understand*
*that by inducing men towards evil,*
*obsessing them and tormenting them,*
*they only prolong their own sufferings.*
*Make the example of the*
*happiness You enjoy into an encouragement for them.*
*Spiritual brother, you who still take pleasure*
*in the practice of evil,*
*listen to the prayer we offer for you,*
*it should convince you that we only desire*
*to help you and not to do you harm.*
*You are unhappy, because it is not possible*
*to be happy while practicing evil.*
*So why do you remain in suffering when the possibility*
*of avoiding it depends on yourself?*
*Look at the good Spirits surrounding you at this moment*
*and see how blessed they are!*
*Would it not be more agreeable for you*
*to enjoy the same happiness?*


*You say this is impossible, however, nothing is impossible*

*to he who wants something,*
*since God gave you, as He did all His creatures,*
*the liberty to choose between good and evil,*
*happiness and wretchedness, and no one*
*is condemned to practice evil.*
*Just as you have the will to do evil,*
*you may also find the will to do good and be happy.*
*Cast your eyes back towards God.*
*Direct your thoughts for an instant to Him*
*and a ray of divine light will illuminate you.*

*Say these simple words together with us:*
*Dear God, I repent, forgive me!*
*Try to repent and do good instead of doing bad things,*
*and you will soon see His mercy*
*descending upon you and an indescribable feeling*
*of well-being will substitute*
*the anguish you experience now.*
*Once you have taken the first step along the pat*
*to goodness the rest of the way will be easy to follow.*
*You will understand then what a long period*
*of happiness you have lost through your own fault.*
*Nevertheless, a radiant future full of hope*
*will open before you and make you forget*
*your miserable past, full of perturbation and moral tortures,*
*which would be hell for you if they were to last for eternity.*
*The day will come when these tortures will be such*
*that you will desire to make them cease at any price.*

Nevertheless, the longer you leave it
the more difficult this will be.
Do not believe that you will always remain
in your present state no,
this is not possible.
You have two prospects before you:
to suffer very much more than you have done until now,
or to be blessed as are the good Spirits who surround you.
The first is inevitable if you persist in being obstinate,
when a simple effort on your part would be sufficient
to take you out of the bad situation
in which you find yourself.
So hurry, seeing that each day you delay
is a lost day of happiness!
Good Spirits, permit these words
to echo in the mind of this backward soul
so they may help him to approach God.
We ask this in the name of Jesus Christ,
Who has such great power over evil Spirits.

# OTHER PRAYERS

## The Litany of the Saints

C- Call

R - Response

**C** - *Lord, have mercy.*

    **R** - *Christ, have mercy.*

**C** - *Lord, have mercy.*

    **R** - *Christ, hear us.*

**C** - *Christ, graciously hear us.*

**C** - *God the Father of Heaven,*

    **R** - *have mercy on us.*

**C** - *God the Son, Redeemer of the world,*

    **R** - *have mercy on us.*

**C** - *God the Holy Spirit,*

    **R** - *have mercy on us.*

**C** - *Holy Trinity, one God,*

    **R** - *have mercy on us.*

**C** - *Holy Mary,*

    **R** - *pray for us.*

**C** - *Holy Mother of God,*

    **R** - *pray for us.*

**C** - *Holy Virgin of virgins,*

    **R** - *pray for us.*

**C** - *St. Michael the Archangel,*

    **R** - *pray for us.*

**C** - *St. Gabriel the Archangel,*

    **R** - *pray for us.*

**C** - *St. Raphael the Archangel,*

    **R** - *pray for us*

**C** - *St. Uriel the Archangel,*

    **R** - *pray for us.*

**C** - *All you holy Angels and Archangels,*

    **R** - *pray for us.*

**C** - *All you holy orders of blessed Spirits,*

    **R** - *pray for us.*

**C** - *St. John the Baptist,*

    **R** - *pray for us.*

**C** - *St. Joseph,*

    **R** - *pray for us.*

**C** - *All you holy Patriarchs and Prophets,*

    **R** - *pray for us.*

**C** - *St. Peter,*

    **R** - *pray for us.*

**C** - *St. Paul,*

    **R** - *pray for us.*

**C** - *St. Andrew,*

    **R** - *pray for us.*

**C** - *St. James,*

    **R** - *pray for us.*

**C** - *St. John,*

    **R** - *pray for us.*

**C** - *St. Thomas,*

    **R** - *pray for us.*

**C** - *St. Philip,*

    **R** - *pray for us.*

**C** - *St. Bartholomew,*

    **R** - *pray for us.*

**C** - *St. Matthew,*

    **R** - *pray for us.*

**C** - *St. Simon,*

    **R** - *pray for us.*

**C** - *St. Thaddeus,*

    **R** - *pray for us.*

**C** - *St. Matthias,*

    **R** - *pray for us.*

**C** - *St. Barnabas,*

    **R** - *pray for us.*

**C** - *St. Luke,*

    **R** - *pray for us.*

**C** - *St. Mark,*

    **R** - *pray for us.*

**C** - *All you holy Apostles and Evangelists,*

    **R** - *pray for us.*

**C** - *All you holy Disciples of the Lord,*

    **R** - *pray for us.*

**C** - *All you holy Innocents,*

    **R** - *pray for us.*

**C** - *St. Stephen,*

    **R** - *pray for us.*

**C** - *St. Lawrence,*

> **R** - *pray for us.*

**C** - *St. Vincent,*

> **R** - *pray for us.*

**C** - *Sts Fabian and Sebastian,*

> **R** - *pray for us.*

**C** - *Sts. John and Paul,*

> **R** - *pray for us.*

**C** - *Sts. Cosmas and Damian,*

> **R** - *pray for us.*

**C** - *St. Sylvester,*

> **R** - *pray for us. All you holy Martyrs,*

**C** - *St. Gregory,*

> **R** - *pray for us.*

**C** - *Saint Barbara*

> **R** - *pray for us.*

**C** - *Saint Lazarus*

> **R** - *pray for us.*

**C** - *Saint Martin of Porres*

> **R** - *pray for us.*

**C** - *St. Martin,*

> **R** - *pray for us.*

**C** - *St. Nicholas,*

> **R** - *pray for us.*

**C** - *Dr. Gregorio and All you holy Doctors,*

> **R** - *pray for us.*

**C** - *St. Anthony,*

> **R** - *pray for us.*

**C** - *St. Benedict,*

> **R** - *pray for us.*

**C** - *St. Bernard,*

> **R** - *pray for us.*

**C** - *St. Francis,*

> **R** - *pray for us.*

**C** - *St. Mary Magdalene,*

> **R** - *pray for us.*

**C** - *Saint Martha*

> **R** - *pray for us.*

**C** - *St. Lucy,*

> **R** - *pray for us.*

**C** - *Saint Cyprian*

> **R** - *pray for us.*

**C** - *St. Cecilia,*

> **R** - *pray for us.*

**C** - *St. Catherine,*

> **R** - *pray for us.*

**C** - *St. Anastasia,*

> **R** - *pray for us.*

**C** - *All you holy Virgins and Widows,*

> **R** - *pray for us.*

**C** - *All you Holy Men and Women, Saints of God,*

> **R** - *make intercession for us.*

**C** - *Be merciful,*

> **R** - *spare us, O Lord.*

**C** - *Be merciful,*

> **R** - *graciously hear us, O Lord.*

**C -** *From all evil, O Lord,*

　**R -** *deliver us.*

**C -** *From all sin,*

　**R -** *deliver us.*

*C -* *From your wrath,*

　**R -** *deliver us.*

**C -** *From sudden and unprovided death,*

　*deliver us.*

**C -** *From the snares of the devil,*

　**R -** *deliver us.*

**C -** *From anger, and hatred, and all ill-will,*

　**R -** *deliver us.*

**C -** *From the spirit of fornication,*

　**R -** *deliver us.*

**C -** *From lightning and tempest,*

　**R -** *deliver us.*

**C -** *From the scourge of earthquake,*

　**R -** *deliver us.*

**C -** *From plague, famine and war,*

　**R -** *deliver us.*

**C -** *From everlasting death,*

　**R -** *deliver us.*

**C -** *Through the mystery of your holy Incarnation,*

　**R -** *deliver us.*

**C -** *Through your Coming,*

　**R -** *deliver us.*

**C -** *Through your Nativity,*

　**R -** *deliver us.*

**C** - *Through your Baptism and holy Fasting,*

    **R** - *deliver us.*

**C** - *Through your Cross and Passion,*

    **R** - *deliver us.*

**C** - *Through your Death and Burial,*

    **R** - *deliver us.*

**C** - *Through your holy Resurrection,*

    **R** - *deliver us.*

**C** - *Through your admirable Ascension,*

    **R** - *deliver us.*

**C** - *Through the coming of the Holy Spirit, the Paraclete, on the day of judgment,*

    **R** - *deliver us.*

**C** - *We sinners,*

    **R** - *we beseech you, hear us.*

**C** - *That you would spare us,*

    **R** - *we beseech you, hear us.*

**C** - *That you would pardon us,*

    **R** - *we beseech you, hear us.*

**C** - *That you would bring us to true penance,*

    **R** - *we beseech you, hear us.*

**C** - *That you would deign to govern and preserve your holy Church,*

    **R** - *we beseech you, hear us.*

**C** - *That you would deign to preserve our Apostolic Prelate, and all orders of the Church in holy religion,*

    **R** - *we beseech you, hear us.*

**C** - *That you would deign to humble the enemies of Holy Church,*

    **R** - *we beseech you, hear us.*

**C** - *That you would deign to give peace and true concord to Christian kings and princes,*

> **R** - *we beseech you, hear us.*

**C** - *That you would deign to grant peace and unity to all Christian people,*

> **R** - *we beseech you, hear us.*

**C** - *That you would deign to call back to the unity of your Grace all who have strayed from the truth and lead all unbelievers to the light of the Gospel,*

> **R** - *we beseech you, hear us.*

**C** - *That you would deign to confirm and preserve us in your holy service,*

> **R** - *we beseech you, hear us.*

**C** - *That you would lift up our minds to heavenly desires,*

> **R** - *we beseech you, hear us.*

**C** - *That you would render eternal blessings to all our benefactors,*

> **R** - *we beseech you, hear us.*

**C** - *That you would deliver our souls and the souls of our brethren, relations and benefactors, from eternal damnation,*

> **R** - *we beseech you, hear us.*

**C** - *That you would deign to give and preserve the fruits of the earth,*

> **R** - *we beseech you, hear us.*

**C** - *That you would deign to grant eternal rest to all the faithful departed,*

> **R** - *we beseech you, hear us.*

**C** - *That you would deign graciously to hear us,*

> **R** - *we beseech you, hear us.*

**C** - *Son of God,*

> **R** - *we beseech you, hear us.*

**C** - *Lamb of God, who take away the sins of the world,*

> **R** - *spare us, O Lord. .*

**C** - *Lamb of God, who take away the sins of the world,*

> **R** - *graciously hear us, O Lord. .*

**C** - *Lamb of God, who take away the sins of the world,*

    **R** - *have mercy on us.*

**C** - *Christ, hear us.*

    **R** - *Christ, graciously hear us.*

**C** - *Lord, have mercy.*

    **R** - *Christ, have mercy.*

**C** - *Lord, have mercy.*

    **R** - *Our Father, etc.(inaudibly).*

**C** - And lead us not into temptation.

    **R** - But deliver us from evil.

**D**eign, O Lord, to rescue me;

O Lord, make haste to help me

Let them be put to shame and confounded who seek my life.

Let them be turned back in disgrace who desire my ruin.

Let them retire in their shame who say to me, "Aha, aha!"

But may all who seek you exult and be glad in you,

And may those who love your salvation say ever,

"God be glorified!"

But I am afflicted and poor;

O God, hasten to me!

You are my help and my deliverer;

O Lord, hold not back!

Glory be to the Father, and to the Son,

and to the Holy Spirit.

As it was in the beginning, is now, and ever shall be,

world without end. Amen.

*Save your servants.*

*Who trust in you, O my God.*

*Be a tower of strength for us, O Lord,*

*Against the attack of the enemy.*

*Let not the enemy prevail against us.*

*And let not the son of evil dare to harm us.*

*O Lord, deal not with us according to our sins.*

*Neither requite us according to our iniquities.*

*Let us pray for our Sovereign Pontiff N.*

*The Lord preserve him, and give him life,*

*and make him blessed upon*

*the earth, and deliver him not up to the will of his enemies.*

*Let us pray for our benefactors.*

*Deign, O Lord, for Your name's sake,*

*to reward with eternal life all*

*those who do us good. Amen.*


*Let us pray for the faithful departed.*

*Eternal rest give to them,*

*O Lord; and let perpetual light shine upon them.*

*May they rest in peace.*

*Amen.*


*For our absent brethren.*

*Save your servants, who trust in you, my God.*

*Send them help, O Lord, from your sanctuary.*

*And sustain them from Zion.*

*O Lord, hear my prayer.*

*And let my cry come to you.*

*The Lord be with you.*

*And with your spirit.*


*Let us pray. O God, whose property is always to have mercy and to spare, receive our petition, that we, and all your servants who are bound by the chains of sin, may, by the compassion of your goodness, be mercifully absolved.*


*Graciously hear, we beg you, O Lord, the prayers of your suppliants, and pardon the sins of those who confess to you, that in your bounty you may grant us both pardon and peace. In your clemency, O Lord, show us your ineffable mercy, that you may both free us from all our sins, and deliver us from the punishments which we deserve for them. O God, who by sin are offended and by penance pacified, mercifully regard the prayers of your suppliant people, and turn away the scourges of your anger,*

*which we deserve for our sins.*


*Almighty, everlasting God, have mercy upon your servant N., our Sovereign Pontiff, and direct him according to your clemency into the way of everlasting salvation, that by your grace he may desire those things that are pleasing to you, and perform them with all his strength.*


*O God, from whom are holy desires, good counsels, and just works, give to your servants that peace which the world cannot give, that our hearts be set to keep your commandments, and that, being removed from the fear of our enemies, we may pass our time in peace under your protection.*


*Burn our desires and our hearts with the fire of the Holy Spirit, O Lord, that we may serve you with a chaste body, and with a clean heart be pleasing to you.*


*O God, the Creator and Redeemer of all the faithful, grant to the souls of your servants and handmaids the remission of all their sins, that, through devout prayers, they may obtain the pardon which they always desired.*

*Direct, we beg you, O Lord, our actions by your holy inspirations, and carry them on by your gracious assistance, that every prayer and work of ours may begin always with you, and through you be happily ended.*

*Almighty and everlasting God, you have dominion over the living and the dead, and you are merciful to all who you foreknow will be yours by faith and good works; we humbly beg you that those for whom we intend to pour forth our prayers, whether this present world still detain them in the flesh, or the world to come has already received them out of their bodies, may, through the intercession of all your Saints, by the clemency of your goodness, obtain the remission of all their sins. Through Christ our Lord.*

*Amen.*

*O Lord, hear my prayer.*

*And let my cry come to you.*

*May the almighty and merciful Lord graciously hear us.*

*Amen.*

*And may the souls of the faithful departed, through the mercy of God,*

*rest in peace.*

*Amen.*

# LITURGY FOR THE DAY OF THE DEAD

O *Just Judge, hear us*

*O Just Judge, graciously hear us.*

*O God the Father of Heaven,*

*O God the Son, Redeemer of the world,*

*O God the Holy Ghost, Perfector of the elect,*

*Holy Trinity, One God*

*Have mercy on the souls of the faithful departed.*

*Holy Mary, Mother of God,*

*To All the Orders of the Blessed Angels,*

*To All the Orders of the Guardian Angels,*

*To All the Orders of the Protective Spirits.*

*To All the Orders of Spirit Guides.*

*To All the Orders of Healing Spirits*

*To all the Orders of Holy Virgins.*

*To all the Saints of God*

*Pray for the souls of the faithful departed.*

*Remember not, O Lord, the offences of Thy servants departed, neither*

*take Thou vengeance on their sins: spare them,*

*good Lord, spare Thy*

*people whom Thou hast redeemed with Thy Most Precious Blood, and be not*
*angry with them for ever.*

*Spare them, good Lord.*

*From all evil,*

*From Thy wrath,*

*From the flames of fire,*

*From the land of the shadow of death,*

*By Thy wonderful Conception,*

*By Thy Holy Nativity and Circumcision,*

*By Thy Most Sweet and Holy Name,*

*Good Lord, deliver them.*

*By Thy Fasting and Temptation,*


*By Thine Agony and Bloody Sweat,*

*By Thy Cross and Passion,*

*By Thy Descent into Hell,*

*By Thy Glorious Resurrection,*

*By Thy Ascension into Heaven,*

*By the Coming of the Holy Ghost,*

*Good Lord, deliver them.*


**C** - *That it may please Thee shortly to accomplish the number of Thine elect, and to hasten Thy kingdom,*

> **R** - *We beseech Thee to hear us.*

**C** - *That it may please Thee to set free our parents, kinsfolk, and friends, from their sins, and from the punishment of them,*

> **R** - *We beseech Thee to hear us.*

**C** - *That it may please Thee to remember and to show mercy, unto all the faithful departed who are not held in remembrance upon earth,*

> **R** - *We beseech Thee to hear us.*

**C** - *That it may please Thee to grant unto all who rest in Christ, a place of refreshment, light and peace.*

> **R** - *We beseech Thee to hear us.*

**C** - *That it may please Thee to wash away all their sins in Thy Most Precious Blood.*

    **R** - *We beseech Thee to hear us.*

**C** - *That it may please Thee, through the prayers and alms of Thy Church, and especially through the Holy Sacrifice of the Mass, to receive them into everlasting habitations,*

    **R** - *We beseech Thee to hear us.*

**C** - *That the Blessed Vision of Jesus may comfort them, and the glorious Light of His Saving Cross shine upon them,*

    **R** - *We beseech Thee to hear us.*

**C** - *That Saint Michael, the standard-bearer, may bring them into the holy light,*

    **R** - *We beseech Thee to hear us.*

**C** - *That Thy Holy Angels may bring them into the land of the living, and the glorious Queen of the Saints, Holy Mary, present them before Thy Throne,*

    **R** - *We beseech Thee to hear us.*

**C** - *O Lamb of God, Who shall come again with glory, to judge both the quick and the dead,*

    **R** - *Grant rest to the souls of the faithful departed.*

**C** - *O Lamb of God, at Whose Presence the earth shall be moved, and the heavens melt away,*

    **R** - *Grant rest to the souls of the faithful departed*

**C** - *O Lamb of God, in Whose Blessed Book of Life, all their names are written,*

    **R** - *Grant rest to the souls of the faithful departed.*


**D**eliver us, O Lord, and all Thy faithful, in that day of terror, when the sun and moon shall be darkened, and the stars fall from heaven: in that day of calamity and amazement, when the heavens shall be shaken, and the pillars of the earth removed, and the glorious majesty of Jesus come, with innumerable Angels, to judge the world by fire.

**C** - *Deliver us, O Lord, in that dreadful day.*

    **R** - *And place us with the Blessed, at Thy right hand for evermore.*

**C** - *O Lord, hear our prayer.*

    **R** - *And let our cry come unto Thee.*


*Let us pray.*


*O God, Whose property is always to have mercy and to forgive: be merciful to the souls of Thy servants and handmaids, and forgive them all their sins, that they, being loosed from the bonds of death, may ascend into the life everlasting, through Jesus Christ our Lord, Who livest and reignest with Thee in the unity of the Holy Spirit, ever one God, world without end.*

Amen.


**C** - *Rest eternal grant unto them, O Lord.*

    **R** - *And let light perpetual shine upon them.*


May they rest in Peace.

Amen.


## Prayer for the Dead


*Death of our dear ones destroys the radiant joy of our home*

*and plunges us in deep distress.*

*We look unto thee, Oh God, for the relief of our grief and comfort of our hearts.*
*Time can soften our sorrow, it cannot efface the loving memory*

*of our dead from our minds.*

*We worship their pious memory and it is the one gleam of sunshine*

*in our lives shadowed by sorrow.*

*The Holy Death has freed them from the material bondage. They have shed their frail earthly clay and departed this life to live hereafter in the realm of the spirit. Their earthly work is done and they have laid down the burden that pressed heavily on them. From the din and dust and storm of life's struggle they have gone to the deathless world of peace and rest where light fades not and happiness fails not. Our beloved have died in body to live in spirit a life higher and nobler than our thoughts can measure and minds can conceive. They rest in everlasting peace and joy with thee.*

*Though lost to us, our dead have not forsaken us.*

*They cannot forget us, as we do not forget them. Though the seven zones divide us and the boundless space part us, they, the spirits, are above and beyond space. They are near us and with us, and see us through our bodily veil. Holy Death has silenced them. They speak not with tongues. They have cast off the vesture of flesh and their souls hold their communion with our souls.*

*They care for us, they feel for us, and they bless us.*

*They long for us and love us, as we long for them and love them.*

*They are ours, as we are theirs.*

*Holy Death has not dissolved our union.*


*Thou has called them to thyself. We commend them into thy hands. Have compassion upon their human infirmities. Absolve them from the errors of their mortal life. If they have sinned in thought and word and deed, spare them in thy mercy. Gather them into thy fold.*

*Admit them in the fellowship of thy blessed dead.*

*Let thy light shine upon them.*

*May they rest in thee in the shining,*

*all-happy paradise of the righteous.*

# Novena for the Holy Souls in Purgatory
## - to illuminate the Souls of the Dead -

**C** - *O most sweet Jesus, through the bloody sweat which Thou didst suffer in the Garden of Gethsemane, have mercy on these Blessed Souls. Have mercy on them.*

    **R** - *Have mercy on them, O Lord.*

**C** - *O most sweet Jesus, through the pains which Thou didst suffer during Thy most cruel scourging, have mercy on them.*

    **R** - *Have mercy on them, O Lord.*

**C** - *O most sweet Jesus, through the pains which Thou didst suffer in Thy most painful crowning with thorns, have mercy on them.*

    **R** - *Have mercy on them, O Lord.*

**C** - *O most sweet Jesus, through the pains which Thou didst suffer in carrying Thy cross to Calvary, have mercy on them.*

    **R** - *Have mercy on them, O Lord.*

**C** - *O most sweet Jesus, through the pains which Thou didst suffer during Thy most cruel Crucifixion, have mercy on them.*

    **R** - *Have mercy on them, O Lord.*

**C** - *O most sweet Jesus, through the pains which Thou didst suffer in Thy most bitter agony on the Cross, have mercy on them.*

    **R** - *Have mercy on them, O Lord.*

**C** - *O most sweet Jesus, through the immense pain which Thou didst suffer in breathing forth Thy Blessed Soul,*

*have mercy on them.*

    **R** - *Have mercy on them, O Lord.*

*Blessed Souls, I have prayed for thee; I entreat thee, who are so dear to God, and who are secure of never losing Him, to pray for me a miserable sinner, who is in danger of being damned, and of losing God forever.*

*Amen.*

# MISA PRAYERS

## The Great Invocation

From the point of Light within the Mind of God
Let light stream forth into the minds of men.
Let Light descend on Earth.

From the point of Love within the Heart of God.
Let love stream forth into the hearts of men.
May Christ return to Earth.

From the centre where the Will of God is known
Let purpose guide the little wills of men—
The purpose which the Masters know and serve.

From the centre which we call the race of men
Let the Plan of Love and Light work out
And may it seal the door where evil dwells.
Let Light and Love and Power restore the Plan on Earth.

# Prayer for the commencement of the Spiritual Meeting

**W**e beseech You, O Lord God, the All Powerful,

to send us the good Spirits to help us and take away all those

who may induce us towards error; give us the necessary light

so that we may distinguish truth from falsity.

Remove too, the maleficent Spirits,

be they incarnate or discarnate, who may try to launch discord amongst us, and
so turn us away from charity and love for our neighbors.

If some of these Spirits try to enter our ambient,

do not allow them access to any of our hearts.

Good Spirits, you see fit to come and teach us,

make us yielding to your counseling,

turn us away from all thoughts of selfishness,

pride, jealousy and envy.

Inspire us to indulgence and benevolence

towards our fellow beings,

present or absent, friends or enemies;

lastly, through the sentiments with which we are animated,

make us recognize Your beneficial influence.

To those Mediums You chose

as transmitters of Your teaching,

give awareness of their mandate and the seriousness

of the act they are about to practice,

so they may perform this act

with the necessary dedication and meditation.

If at our meeting, there be any persons present

*driven by sentiments other than those of goodness,*

*open their eyes to the light and forgive them Lord,*

*as we forgive them, for any evil intentions they may harbor.*

*We ask especially that the Spirit of X..., who is our spiritual Guide, assist us and watch over us.*

## Prayer for the Mediums

A*lmighty God,*

*permit the good Spirits to come*

*and help me in the communication that is solicited.*

*Protect me from the presumption of judging myself*

*to be safe from evil Spirits,*

*from the pride which may induce me to err*

*with respect to the value of what I receive,*

*from all sentiments which are the opposite of charity*

*towards other mediums.*

*If I fall into error inspire someone to alert me of this fact;*

*and give me the humility that will enable me*

*to accept the deserved criticism and to recognise*

*that the advice the good Spirits wish to give through me*

*is not only addressed to others, but primarily to myself.*

*If I am tempted to abuse in whatever form,*

*the faculty whose bestowal You approved,*

*or to become proud of it,*

*I ask that You take it back*

*rather than it be permitted to stray*

*from its providential objective,*

*which is for the good of all and my own moral betterment.*


## To The Guardian Angels and Protecting Spirits


**W**ise and benevolent Spirits, messengers of God,

*whose mission is to help Man*

*and conduct him towards goodness,*

*uphold me in life's tests; give me the strength to suffer without complaining; turn away from me all evil thoughts, and do not allow me to give access to any bad Spirits who may try to induce me to evil.*

*Clarify my conscience with respect to my defects,*

*and take away the veil of pride from my eyes which can*

*prevent my seeing them and admitting them to myself.*

*Particularly to X. . ., my Guardian Angel, who watches over me specially; and all the rest of you protecting Spirits who take an interest in me,*

*I beg you to help me to become worthy of your protection.*

*You know my needs; may they be attended to*

*according to the Will of God.*

## Prayer for the Guardian Angel and Spirit Guide

**D**ear God,

*allow the good Spirits who accompany me*
*to help me when I am in difficulty*
*and uphold me when I falter.*
*Lord, may they inspire me with faith,*
*hope and charity; may they be a point of support,*
*an inspiration and a testimony of Your mercy.*
*In short, may I always encounter in them*
*the strength that I lack for the tests of life,*
*the strength to resist all evil suggestions,*
*the faith that saves and the love that consoles.*


## Another Prayer for the Guardian Angel and Spirit Guide

**B**eloved Spirits and Guardian Angels,

*who God in His infinite mercy has permitted*
*to assist mankind,*
*be our protectors during all life's tests!*
*Give us the necessary strength, courage and resignation,*
*inspire us towards all that is good,*
*and restrain us from the downward incline to evil,*
*may your sweet influences fill our souls,*
*make us feel that a devoted friend is by our side,*

*who can see our suffering and who participates*

*in all our joys. And you, my Good Angel,*

*never abandon me because I need all of your protection*

*to be able to support with faith and love*

*the tests that God has sent me.*

## Prayer to turn away the bad spirits

*In the Name of God the All Powerful,*

*may the bad Spirits turn away from me*

*and the good Spirits defend me from them!*

*Wicked Spirits, who inspire bad thoughts in men;*

*deceiving and lying Spirits, who delude men,*

*mocking Spirits, who amuse yourselves*

*with mankind's incredulity,*

*I repel you with all the strength within my soul*

*and close my ears to your suggestions,*

*but I also implore that God's mercy be upon you.*

*Good Spirits, who undertook to accompany me,*

*give me the necessary strength to resist*

*the influence of bad Spirits and the necessary enlightenment*

*so as not to become a victim of their intrigue.*

*Safeguard me from pride and presumption.*

*We ask that you turn aside all thoughts of jealousy,*

*hate, badness, and all sentiments contrary*

*to charity from my heart,*

*which are all as open doors to the bad Spirits*

## Prayer to Close a Spiritual Meeting

*We give thanks to the good Spirits*
*who have come to communicate with us,*
*and implore them to help us put into practice*
*the instructions they have given, and also,*
*that on leaving this ambient, they may help us*
*to feel strengthened for the practice of goodness*
*and love towards our fellow beings.*
*We also desire that Your teachings help all those*
*Spirits who are suffering, ignorant or corrupt,*
*who have participated in our meeting*
*and for whom we implore God's mercy.*

# SOME SONGS FOR MISA ESPIRITUAL

## Sea el Santísimo

Sea el Santísimo ... Sea

Sea el Santísimo ... Sea

¡Madre mía de la caridad!

Ayúdanos , ampáranos

En el nombre de Dios ...

¡Ay Dios!


Si la luz redentora te llama, buen ser,

y te llama con amor a la tierra,

yo quisiera ver a ese ser

cantándole al verbo

al divino Manuel.


Oye buen ser,

avanza y ven,

que el coro te llama

y te dice ven.


¡ay ,buen ser!

avanza y ven

que el coro te llama

y te dice ven.

Allá a lo lejos se ve,

se ve bajar una luz,

es la Virgen María
que viene a ver
esta coronación ...
Es la Virgen María
que viene a ver
esta coronación ...

En coronación , en coronación,
bajan los seres ...
En coronación , en coronación,
bajan los seres ...
Oh , venid protectores , venid,
seres guías de nuestra misión
Oh venid protectores a la tierra
a ver que linda coronación.

Comisión despojadora,
comisión que aquí llego,
santiguando y despojando,
despojando en nombre de Dios

## Oreen

Oreen, oreen, oreen, oreen,
Oreen hermanos míos oreen,
Oreen para ese ser.
Del cielo ha bajado, la madre de Dios,
cantemos el Ave Maria con amor,

ave, ave, Ave maria.

ave, ave, ave Maria

Se repite

## San Salvador

Bendícelo San Salvador,

San Salvador bendícelo,

bendícelo en nombre de Dios.

Hay bendícelo San Salvador,

San Salvador bendícelo

En nombre de Dios

## Oh , venid protectores

Oh , venid protectores , venid,

Seres guías de nuestra misión.

Oh venid protectores a la tierra

A ver que linda coronación.

## En coronación

En coronación , en coronación,

bajan los seres.

En coronación , en coronación

bajan los seres.

Santa Clara, aclaradora,

aclara a este humilde ser

que viene de lo infinito,

buscando la claridad

Santa Clara , aclaradora,

aclara a este humilde ser

que viene de lo infinito

lo queremos conocer.


Si a tu puerta llama un ser

pidiendo la caridad ...

No se la niegues , hermano,

que dios te lo pagará.


### San Lázaro

Siete días, con siete noches,

por el mundo caminando,

y no encuentro una limosna,

para mi viejo Babalu Aye

Tanto como yo camino,

tanto como yo trabajo,

y no encuentro una limosna,

para mi viejo Babalu Aye

Babalu Aye, Babalu Aye, Babalu aye

Dadme diecisiete céntimos

Para Babalu ayeeeeeee


Marinero , marinero,

marinero de alta mar:

préstame tu barquillita

para irme a navegar.

Si yo fuera marinero,

marinero de verdad

te prestaría mi barquilla

para irme a navegar.

A Remar ,a remar ,a remar,

A Remar ,a remar ,a remar,

A Remar ,a remar ,a remar,

Que a Virgen de Regla nos va a acompañar.

## Canción a Mama Francisca

Siento una voz que me llama

de lo profundo del mar

y es la voz de una africana

que viene a elaborar;

y yo llamo a mi madre y no viene,

y yo llamo a mi padre y tampoco,

yo llamo a mi seres guías,

que vengan poquito a poco,

Mama Francisca te estoy llamando, hay Dios

Mama Francisca en nombre de Dios

Mama Francisca, Reina Africana

Reina Africana del Lucumi

## Congo de Guinea

Congo de Guinea soy ...

Buenas noches criollos ...

Congo de Guinea soy ...

Buenas noches criollos ...

Yo dejé mi hueso allá,

yo vine a hacer caridad.


Congo de Guinea soy ...

Buenas noches criollos ...

Congo de Guinea soy ...

Buenas noches criollos ...

Yo dejé mi hueso allá,

yo vine a hacer caridad.


Congo , conguito

Congo de verdad ...

yo baja a la tierra

a hacer caridad ...


Congo , conguito

Congo de verdad ...

Yo baja a la tierra

a hacer caridad ...

Congo bueno , ngangulero,

Ven y afirma tu fundamento ...

Congo bueno , ngangulero,

Ven y afirma tu fundamento ...

Indio Rojo, Indio Caribe,

yo te llamoa labora.

Indio Rojo, Indio Caribe.

yo te llamo a laborar

Vamo a ve , vamo a ve

vamo a ve si son verdad,

si son congo o no son congo

si son congo , son nganga.


Vamo a ve , vamo a ve

vamo a ve si son verdad,

si son congo o no son congo

si son congo , son nganga.


Congo de Guinea soy

Buenas noches criollo

Buenas noches criollo

Yo dejo mi huesa allá

Yo vengo hacer caridad

Yo dejo mi huesa allá

Yo vengo hacer caridad


Congo conguito congo de verdad

Tú vas a la tierra hacer caridad

Congo conguito congo de verdad

Tú vas a la tierra hacer caridad

Yo dejo mi huesa allá
Yo vengo hacer caridad
Yo dejo mi huesa aya
Yo vengo hacer caridad

Pa que tú me llamas
Pa que tú me llamas
Si tú no me conoces
Pa que tú me llamas
Pa que tú me llamas
Si tú no me conoces
Pa que tú me llamas
Pa que tú me llamas
Pa que tú me llamas
Si tú no me conoces

Yo soy un negro congo
Pa que tú me llamas
Pa que tú me llamas
Pa que tú me llamas
Si tú no me conoces

Yo vengo piango, piango
Pa que tú me llamas
Pa que tú me llamas
Pa que tú me llamas
Si tú no me conoces

Yo vengo de los montes

Pa que tú me llamas

Pa que tú me llamas

Pa que tú me llamas

Si tú no me conoces


Yo vengo derechito

Pa que tú me llamas

Pa que tú me llamas

Pa que tú me llamas

Si tú no me conoces


Yo vengo a elaborar

Pa que tú me llamas

Pa que tú me llamas

Pa que tú me llamas .

# OTHER SPIRITUAL PRACTICES

## Novena to Saint Anthony

Recite these prayers for 9 consecutive days...

O *Glorious St Anthony,*
*Charitable Protector of all who call upon you,*
*with filial trust I cast myself on your mercy.*
*Look upon the misery that oppresses me,*
*and by your intercession appease the anger of God,*
*whom I have offended by my sins.*
*Deliver me from the affliction*
*that I may serve Him with a mind of peace.*

*At the same time should this suffering*

*be expedient for my salvation,*

*I desire to be resigned asking you*

*to obtain for me constant patience*

*and entire conformity to the will of Him Who*

*for love of us being Himself innocent*

*gave satisfaction for the guilty.*

*I beseech you not to forsake me in my misfortunes*

*and by you merits our dear Lord*

*may strengthened us in His service,*

*console us in our afflictions and finally give us grace so to live*

*as to be worthy of life everlasting to praise,*

*bless and love Him in your company*

*for ever and ever.*

*Amen.*

# The Litany of St Anthony

## Preface:

C - *Lord have mercy on us All:*

    R - *Christ have mercy on us.*

C - *Lord have mercy on us.*

    R - *Christ hear us Christ graciously hear us.*

C - *God, the Father of Heaven,*

    R - *Have mercy on us.*

C - *God the Son Redeemer of the world,*

    R - *Have Mercy on us.*

C - *God the Holy Spirit,*

    R - *Have mercy on us.*

C - *Holy Trinity One God,*

    R - *Have mercy on us.*

*Holy Mary,*

    R - *Pray for us.*

C - *Holy Mother of God,*

    R - *Pray for us.*

C - *Holy Virgin of Virgins,*

    R - *Pray for us.*

C - *St Joseph, spouse of Mary,*

    R - *Pray for us.*

C - *St Francis, Patriarch of the poor,*

    R - *Pray for us.*

C - *St Anthony of Padua,*

    R - *Pray for us.*

**C** - *St Anthony, friend of Jesus and Mary,*

    **R** - *Pray for us.*

**C** - *St Anthony, apostolic man,*

    **R** - *Pray for us.*

**C** - *St Anthony, filled with the Spirit of prophecy,*

    **R** - *Pray for us.*

**C** - *St Anthony, sublime doctor of truth,*

    **R** - *Pray for us.*

**C** - *St Anthony, ornament of the seraphic order,*

    **R** - *Pray for us.*

**C** - *St Anthony, light of Holy Church,*

    **R** - *Pray for us.*

**C** - *St Anthony, preacher of grace,*

    **R** - *Pray for us.*

**C** - *St Anthony, trumpet of Gospel,*

    **R** - *Pray for us.*

**C** - *St Anthony, mirror of regular observance,*

    **R** - *Pray for us.*

**C** - *St Anthony, cultivator of a mortified life,*

    **R** - *Pray for us.*

**C** - *St Anthony, medal of abstinence,*

    **R** - *Pray for us.*

**C** - *St Anthony, example of obedience,*

    **R** - *Pray for us.*

**C** - *St Anthony, lover of poverty,*

    **R** - *Pray for us.*

**C** - *St Anthony, lily of chastity,*

    **R** - *Pray for us.*

**C** - *St Anthony, rose of patience,*

    **R** - *Pray for us.*

**C** - *St Anthony, brilliant gem of sanctity,*

    **R** - *Pray for us.*

**C** - *St Anthony, violet of humility,*

    **R** - *Pray for us.*

**C** - *St Anthony, hammer of heresy,*

    **R** - *Pray for us.*

**C** - *St Anthony, fervent in zeal for Divine worship,*

    **R** - *Pray for us.*

**C** - *St Anthony, thirsting for the salvation of souls,*

    **R** - *Pray for us.*

**C** - *St Anthony, Martyr in desire,*

    **R** - *Pray for us.*

**C** - *St Anthony, lover and assiduous imitator of the Redeemer,*

    **R** - *Pray for us.*

**C** - *St Anthony, devout client of the Virgin,*

    **R** - *Pray for us.*

**C** - *Mother of God,*

    **R** - *Pray for us.*

**C** - *St Anthony, emulator of the seraphic Francis,*

    **R** - *Pray for us.*

**C** - *Lamb of God who takes away the sins of the world,*

    **R** - *Spare us O Lord.*

**C** - *Lamb of God who takes away the sins of the world,*

    **R** - *Graciously hear us O Lord.*

**C** - *Lamb of God who takes away the sins of the world,*

    **R** - *Have mercy on us.*

## Novena to Saint Michael the Archangel

Glorious Saint Michael,

guardian and defender
of the Church of Jesus Christ,
come to the assistance of His followers,
against whom the powers of hell are unchained.
Guard with special care our Holy Father,
the Pope, and our bishops, priests,
all our religious and lay people,
and especially the children.

*Saint Michael,*
*watch over us during life,*
*defend us against the assaults of the demon,*
*and assist us especially at the hour of death.*
*Help us achieve the happiness*
*of beholding God face to face*
*for all eternity.*

*Amen.*

*Saint Michael,*
*intercede for me with God*
*in all my necessities, especially*

(State your intention here...)

*Obtain for me a favorable outcome*
*in the matter I recommend to you.*
*Mighty prince of the heavenly host,*
*and victor over rebellious spirits,*
*remember me for I am weak and sinful*
*and so prone to pride and ambition.*
*Be for me, I pray,*
*my powerful aid in temptation and difficulty,*
*and above all do not forsake me*
*in my last struggle with the powers of evil.*

# Novena to Saint Martha

**Preface:** The prayer that follows must be recited for nine consecutive Tuesdays, lighting a candle on each Tuesday. This miraculous Saint has been known to grant anything, no matter how difficult it is, before the ninth Tuesday.

$S$*aint Martha,*

*I resort to thy aid and protection.*

*As proof of my affection and faith,*

*I offer thee this light,*

*which I shall burn every Tuesday.*

*Comfort me in all my difficulties*

*and through the great favors thou didst enjoy*

*when the Savior was lodged in thy house,*

*intercede for my family,*

*that we be provided for in our necessities.*

*I ask of thee, Saint Martha,*

*to overcome all difficulties*

*as thou didst overcome the dragon*

*which thou hadst at thy feet.*

*In the name of the Father*

*and of the Son and of the Holy Spirit.*


*Amen*


Recite the following prayers...

> *Our Father...*
>
> *Hail Mary...*
>
> *Glory Be...*


Saint Martha is often used in work to dominate another - be it a judge, miserable boss or wandering lover. In any circumstance where you need to exert your will or influence over another, you can set this lamp for Saint Martha. In this manifestation, she becomes Martha Dominadora.

You will need:

> -1 Red Onion, Sliced
> -Five Senses Oil
> -Saint Martha Perfume
> -Red Palm Oil
> -5 Bay Leaves
> -Brown Sugar
> -Red Clover Herb
> -Commanding Powder

-Red Ribbon
-Wicking Material
-Castor Oil
-Saint Martha Amulet
-Dragon's Blood Ink
-Brown Paper
-Personal items of target - hair, signature, photo, footprint dirt, etc.(if available)
-Medium Size Glass Bowl

## Directions:

Write the full name of your target nine times on brown paper in dragon's blood ink. Cover the name with a command written nine times. Roll up the name paper and tie it with red ribbon. Moving back and forth from left to right, make 4 more knots in the ribbon – there should be five knots total - including the one holding the rolled name paper.

Put the following lamp ingredients in the glass container, on top of the name paper roll and personal items if available.

1 sliced red onion
5 drops of St Martha Perfume
5 drops 5 senses Oil
3 teaspoons Red Palm Oil
Saint Martha Amulet
1 teaspoon brown sugar
5 Bay Leaves
Pinch of Red Clover Herb
Commanding Powder

Prepare your wick and fill with Castor Oil. Light the lamp on a Tuesday in front of the image of Saint Martha (there is one on the package the amulet arrives in).

Say this prayer to Saint Martha five times for nine nights:


**H**oly Virgin Saint Martha,
Who entered the mountain and tied
Up the beast with your ribbons,
I beg you to tie up and dominate [insert name of target].


Saint Martha,
Let him/her not sit in a chair,
Nor lie in a bed until he/she is at my feet.
Holy Martha, hear me,
Help Me for the love of God.


Holy Virgin Martha,
For the oil which you will consume today,
For the oil which nourishes this lamp,
For the wick which burns away all impurities,
I dedicate this Lamp to you,
So that you may relieve me
Of all my Miseries
And Help Me to Overcome all Difficulties.
As You dominated the beast at your feet,
Give me Health and Work
So that I may provide for my needs.


My Mother,
Grant me that [insert target's name here]
May not live in Peace,
Until he/she comes to stand at my feet.
In this way my Mother,
For the Love of God
Grant my Petition and Eliminate My Misery.
Amen."

Tend to the lamp by adding more Base Oil and Red Palm Oil daily as it burns. Add more perfume as needed to scent the lamp. After nine nights, remove the wick and add it to a Commanding Bath. Extract the Saint Martha Amulet and wear it around your waist tie on a red ribbon. Dispose of the rest of the lamp at the crossroads of a Catholic Church.

# Other Novenas

## The Infant Jesus of Prague

Feast day: December 25 / Mondays

Use Orange or Red 7 day candles

Invoked for: Health, surgery, guidance, wisdom, special requests.

## The Infant Jesus of Atocha

Feast day: December 25 / Mondays

Use Gold or Yellow 7 day candles

Invoked for: Health, law matters, court matters.

## Our Lady of Fatima

Feast day: May 13 / Tuesdays

Use White 7 day candles

Invoked for: Protection against evil, freedom from binding situations.

## Our Lady of Grace

Feast day: January 21 / Fridays

Use Blue 7 day candles

Invoked for: Special requests, calming anger, finding love, fidelity in marriage.

## Our Lady of Guadelupe

Feast day: December 12 / First of the month

Use Pink, white or 3 colors green, white, red 7 day candles

Invoked for: Peace, health, general help, luck for the month.

## Our Lady of Charity

Feast day: September 8 / Saturdays

Use Yellow 7 day candles

Invoked for: Protection of home and family, return love or bring new love, money.


## Our Lady of the Immaculate Conception

Feast day: December 8 / Mondays

Use White 7 day candles

Invoked for: Help in sickness, general health, fertility.


## Our Lady of Loretto

Feast day: December 10 / Saturdays

Use White 7 day candles

Invoked for: Help in finding a place to live, protection when traveling by plane, peace in the home. Patroness of Aviators.


## Our Lady of Lourdes

Feast day: February 11 / Wednesdays

Use White 7 day candles

Invoked for: Help to regain health, special favors.


## Our Lady of Mercy

Feast day: September 24 / Sundays

Use White 7 day candles

Invoked for: Needed justice, release from jail.

## Our Lady of the Miraculous Medal

Feast day: November 27 / Wednesdays

Use Blue and White 7 day candles

Invoked for: Health, break bad habits, avert danger, special favors.


## Our Lady of Hope

Feast day: August 1 / Thursdays

Use Blue 7 day candles

Invoked for: Overcoming enemies, protection in times of war.


## Our Lady of Perpetual Help

Feast day: March 7 / Sundays

Use White or Blue 7 day candles

Invoked for: Protection of Children.


## Our Lady of Relga

Feast day: September 7 / Fridays

Use Blue 7 day candles

Invoked for: Protection of children, fertility, money problems.


## Our Lady of Mount Carmel

Feast day: July 16 / Saturdays

Use White or Brown 7 day candles

Invoked for: Protection from accidents or sudden death.

## Our Lady of Prompt Succor

Feast day: August 1 / Saturdays

Use Gold candles

Invoked for: Epidemics, sickness, to bring change. Patroness of Louisiana

## Saint Agnes

Feast day: January 21 / Fridays

Use White or Blue 7 day candles

Invoked for: Problems concerning fertility, to find a mate, sincerity in relationships

## Saint Anne/Ann/Ana

Feast day: July 26 / Mondays

Use White 7 day candles

Invoked for: Help for the Blind or Deaf, also to find a husband

## Saint Barbara

Feast day: December 4 / Saturdays

Use Red 7 day candles

Invoked for: Drive away evil, protector of women, love problems, protection during storms. Patroness of Storms, builders, architects, artillery.

## Saint Maria Goretti

Feast day: July 6 / Fridays

Use Pink 7 day candles

Invoked for: Concerning fidelity in marriage, abusive relationships.

## Saint Brigid(Bride) of Kildare

Feast day: February 1 / Sundays

Use Yellow 7 day candles or a cow candle

Invoked for: Childbirth, protection from fire, fertility, love, animals, husbandry.


## Saint Claire of Assasi

Feast day: August 11 / Mondays

Use White 7 day candles

Invoked for: Protection against evils of body and soul, help with drug or alcohol problems.


## Saint Catherine of Alexandria

Feast day: November 25/ Saturdays

Use Yellow or White 7 day candles

Invoked for: Beauty, fertility, love, femininity, jealousy, healing, visions and dreams. Patroness of teachers, jurors, philosophers.


## Saint Dymphna

Feast day: May 15 / Mondays

Use Blue 7 day candles

Invoked for: Insanity, obsession, demons, nervous disorders, mental afflictions, family.


## Saint Cecilia

Feast day: November 22 / Wednesdays

Use Green or Organ 7 day candles

Invoked for: Success for composers, organ makers, poets, singers, also the patroness of the above listed.

## Saint Francis Xavier Cabrini

Feast day: November 13 / Sundays

Use White 7 day candles

Invoked for: Health, education.


## Saint Helen of Jerusalem

Feast day: August 18 / Fridays

Use Pink or Red 7 day candles

Invoked for: Love, return love, overcome sadness. Patroness of archaeologists.


## Saint Joan of Arc

Feast day: May 30 / Tuesday

Use Grey 7 day candles

Invoked for: To overcome enemies, for courage, freedom from containing situations. Patroness of France


## Saint Lucy

Feast day: December 13 / Wednesdays

Use White 7 day candles

Invoked for: Eye problems, legal problems, temptations.


## Saint Martha

Feast day: July 29 / Tuesdays

Use Green and White 7 day candles

Invoked for: Money problems, domestic problems, to draw love, keep partner faithful, beat enemies. Patroness of happy homes, housekeepers, dieticians, innkeepers.

## Saint Philomena

Feast day: August 11 / Saturdays

Use Pink or Green 7 day candles

Invoked for: Support expectant mothers, child problems, unhappiness in the home, sterility, the sick, money problems, mental illness.

## Saint Rita of Cascia

Feast day: May 22 / Sundays

Use White 7 day candles

Invoked for: Against loneliness, abusive relationships, healing wounds, tumors. Patroness of hopeless cases.

## Saint Therese of Lisieux

Feast day: October 1 / Wednesdays

Use Yellow or Roses 7 day candles

Invoked for: Drug and alcohol problems, protection from enemies using black magic.

## Saint Anthony of Padua

Feast day: June 13 / Tuesdays

Depends on the Request, green for money, brown for special requests, orange for marriage

Invoked for: To find lost items, improve memory, marital or love problems, bring back strayed love, overcome financial problems.

## Saint Alphonsus Liguori

Feast day: August 1 / Thursdays

Use Purple 7 day candles

Invoked for: Rheumatic fever, arthritis, gout, ailments that afflict joints or muscles or bones.

## Saint Aloysius

Feast day: June 21 / Wednesdays

Use Blue 7 day candles

Invoked for: Cases for fevers, epidemics and plagues.

## Saint Bartholomew

Feast day: August 24 / Tuesdays

Use Red 7 day candles

Invoked for: Truth, protection against violence, surgery.

## Saint Benedict

Feast day: July 11 / Saturdays

Use White 7 day candles

Invoked for: Protection against infectious disease, Safe labor, healing sick animals, assistance at a time of death.

## Saint Alex/Alexis/San Alejo

Feast day: July 17 / Sundays

Use Pink 7 day candles

Invoked for: To keep enemies away, protection from enemies.

## Saint Blaise/Blas

Feast day: February 3 / Wednesdays

Use Blue 7 day candles

Invoked for: Disease in humans and animals, the throat, communications.

## Saint Florian

Feast day: May 4/ Sundays

Use Red or Orange 7 day candles

Invoked for: Protect the home against fire, protection from danger.

## Saint Christopher

Feast day: July 25 / Wednesdays

Use Red 7 day candles

Invoked for: Against impenitence at death, protection against accidents, sudden death, for safe travel and to cure contagious diseases.

## Saints Cosmas & Damian

Feast day: September 27/ Wednesdays

Use 2 Green 7 day candles

Invoked for: Health matters, sicknes, fight on your behalf, overcome obstacles.

## Saint Cipriano

Feast day: October 9 / Saturdays

Use Purple 7 day candles

Invoked for: Travel, for homeless people, against harm, bad neighbors, cheats and liars.

## Saint Expedite

Feast day: April 19 / Thursdays

Yellow and Purple 7 day candles

Invoked for: To settle disputes, for help in working death spells or curses, and to bring change.


## Saint Gerard Majella

Feast day: October 16 / Mondays

Use White 7 day candles

Invoked for: To become pregnant, for expectant mothers, when falsely accused, ecstasies, channeling, prophecy, mediumship, healing


## Saint Francis of Assasi

Feast day: October 4 / Mondays

Use Brown 7 day candles

Invoked for: Peace, detection of evil plots, animals, conservation. Patron Saint of animals, birds,


## Saint George

Feast day: April 23 / Tuesdays

Use Red 7 day candles

Invoked for: To conquer fear, overcome jealousy, skin problems.


## Saint Ignatius of Loyola

Feast day: July 31 / Saturdays

Use White 7 day candles

Invoked for: Protect the home from intruders, and from evil spirits.

## Saint James the Greater

Feast day: July 25 / Tuesdays

Use Red 7 day candles

Invoked for: To conquer enemies, for justice.


## Saint Joachim

Feast day: July 26/ Fridays

Use Green 7 day candles

Invoked for: To find a faithful husband.


## Saint John the Baptist

Feast day: June 24 / Tuesdays

Use Green 7 day candles

Invoked for: Good luck, crops, fertility and protection against enemies.


## Saint John Bosco

Feast day: January 31 / Sundays

Use Yellow 7 day candles

Invoked for: Temporal needs, problems with children and for students.


## Saint Joseph

Feast day: March 19 / Sundays

Use Yellow and Lilac 7 day candles

Invoked for: Protection, happy death, finding employment, sell a home, end famine, for married couples.

## Saint Jude

Feast day: October 28 / Sundays

Use Red, White and Green 7 day candles

Invoked for: Hopeless or impossible cases, help against drug addictions, to get out of jail.

## Saint Lazarus

Feast day: December 17 / Sundays

Use Yellow 7 day candles

Invoked for: The sick, crippled and help against drug addictions, prosperity.

## Saint Martin de Porres

Feast day: November 3 / Thursdays

Use Purple and White 7 day candles

Invoked for: Financial needs, health, harmony.

## Saint Martin of Tours,(Saint Martin Caballero)

Feast day: November 11 / Tuesdays

Use Red and White 7 day candles

Invoked for: Against evil and enemies, and evil influences, business, money, luck, prosperity.

## Saint Patrick

Feast day: March 17 / Sundays

Use White 7 day candles

Invoked for: Against snakebite, for prosperity, luck, spiritual wisdom and guidance. Patron Saint of Ireland.

## Saint Paul

Feast day: June 29 / Tuesdays

Use Blue or Red 7 day candles

Invoked for: To overcome opposition, for courage, for unsettled home.

## Saint Peter

Feast day: June 29 / Tuesdays

Use Red and White 7 day candles

Invoked for: Success, to remove obstacles, better business, good fortune.

## Saint Peregrine

Feast day: May 1 or 2 / Sundays

Use White 7 day candles

Invoked for: Health problems involving cancer.

## Saint Pius the Tenth

Feast day: August 21 / Sundays

Use White 7 day candles

Invoked for: Special requests, favors granted from those in authority.

## Saint Raymond Nonnatus

Feast day: August 31 / Tuesdays

Red 7 day candles

Invoked for: To stop gossip, protection of unborn babies.

## Saint Louis Bertrand

Feast day: October 9 / any day

Use White 7 day candles

Invoked for: Protection against evil, sickness and from enemies, invoke to remove malochia from children.


## Saint Roch or Roque

Feast day: August 16 / Wednesdays

Use Yellow 7 day candles

Invoked for: To restore health after fevers.


## Saint Sebastian

Feast day: January 20/ Tuesdays

Red 7 day candles

Invoked for: Justice, court cases, to overcome rivals, obstacles, for success and good fortune.


## Saint Thomas Aquinas

Feast day: January 28 / Mondays

Use White 7 day candles

Invoked for: To improve memory and when sitting exams.


## Guardian Angel

Feast day: Mondays

Use White 7 day candles

Invoked for: Against the evil eye, for spiritual strength

## Saint Raphael the Archangel

Feast day: September 29 / any day

Use Pink 7 day candles

Invoked for: Safe journey, reunited with loved ones, to cure all sickness, keep out evil spirits, to protect from possession of evil spirits, and in any time of need.


## Saint Michael the Archangel

Feast day: September 29 / any day

Use Red, Purple & Green 7 day candles

Invoked for: Deliverance from enemies, protection from evil, victory, protection of the home and business.

# SOME OTHER PRAYERS

## Prayer to La Negra Madama

Oh Holy Spirit of La Negra Madama.
I implore your sublime influences,
for my protection..
By the Virtue of Oloddumare, Olofi and Olorun.
I ask you to help and guide me.
Oh Grand Spirit of La Madama, give me courage!
Use your Divine Wisdom,
and your Divine influences, so
that no Man nor Woman,
under the eyes of God, may harm me. I ask
this with Pure Respect,
Pure faith, and Pure Homage!! Ibae!!
Ashe-O!

## Prayer to the Congo Spirit

O *glorious black spirit,*
*For your virtues you have reached the Holy Blessings of God,*
*And have come to the heavenly court*
*To be surrounded by Angels and Archangels.*

*I, an admirer of your strength,*
*knowledge and great kindness, ask in the name of God,*
*That you fill my body with your invisible power*
*To separate from me the evil thoughts*
*That my enemies may want to send me.*

*Free me, my Congo, from all evil spirits.*
*Tie their feet, hands, and all evil thoughts.*

*Oh, great Congo Spirit,*
*With your help I will defeat my enemies.*
*With your invisible powers I will be blessed*
*With the Holy power God has given you.*
*You, oh great Congo will help me in all my needs.*

*I ask, oh Congo Spirit, divine protector that you guard*
*the surroundings of my home against envy,*
*jealousy, and bad faith.*
*Free me, my Congo of all bad influences*
*and do not abandon me. Amen*

## Prayer to the Aloe

Virtuous Aloe, Blessed Aloe ,Holy Aloe, Sacred Aloe;

through your virtue that you gave to the Apostles

I ask that you extend to me this virtue

because I venerate you and I love you

so that you may free me

from Evil Acts, Sickness, Bad Luck,

that my businesses do well,

in business transactions and that you drive evil

away from my home

and you free me from enemies everywhere I may go:

that you may give me work, Blessings, Fortune and Money

with all ease and the least effort,

your virtue will make me strong, famous,

fortunate and joyous,

do not place obstacles in all that I am ambitious for,

desire or propose to do, make for me a flattering success;

this virtue divine that God gave you,

in God I believe and in you I trust.


Through all of the virtues that you concede to me

I will defeat all of the obstacles that are presented to me

and my home will fill with blessings with your virtue sublime and portentous
Holy Aloe.

## Prayer to the Door

**D***ivine Providence,*

*you who were the author of all that I believe without whose will nothing is
moved, I think of you in my moments of uncertainty so that you
will guide me and protect me from evil and envious spirits.*

*Guide me my spirit, if any of my enemies raise their hands to hurt me or says
something to harm me, turn aside their hands and their evil thoughts, and have
them ask my pardon. And I will forgive them and beg God for their salvation.
Guardian Angel, do not let me become a victim or be blamed for sins I have
not committed for the satisfaction my enemies want from experimenting with
false and obscure spirits.*

*In the name of the All Powerful God, I beg my Guardian Angel and the
spirits that protect me that I be freed from all bad influences and temptation
and that those false and seductive spirits will not enter my body or my house and
that the spirits of light will save me forever.*

*Great Power as I place this prayer over the entrance to my home let it be a wall
to my material and spiritual enemies.*

*Amen*

## Ashanti Prayer for Blessing

O *Lord, O God,*

*creator Of Our land, our earth, the trees,*

*the animals and humans, all is for your honor*

*The drums beat it out, and people sing about it,*

*and they dance with noisy joy that you are the Lord.*

*You also have pulled the other continents out of the sea.*

*What a wonderful world you have made out of the wet mud,*

*and what beautiful men and women!*

*We thank you for the beauty of this earth.*

*The grace of your creation is like a cool day between rainy seasons.*

*We drink in your creation with our eyes.*

*We listen to the birds' jubilee with our ears.*

*How strong and good and sure your earth smells, and everything that grows there.*

*The sky above us is like a warm, soft Kente cloth, because you are behind it,*

*else it would be cold and rough and uncomfortable.*

*We drink in your creation and cannot get enough of it.*

*But in doing this we forget the evil we have done.*

*Lord, we call you, we beg you:*

*tear us away from our sins and our death.*

*This wonderful world fades away.*

*And one day our eyes snap shut, and all is over and dead that is not from you.*

*We are still slaves of the demons and the fetishes of this earth.*

*When we are not saved by you.*

*Bless us.*

*Bless our land and people.*

*Bless our forests with mahogany, wawa, and cacao.*

*Bless our fields with cassava and peanuts.*

*Bless the waters that flow through our land.*

*Fill them with fish and drive great schools of fish to our seacoast,*

*so that the fishermen in their unsteady boats do not need to go out too far.*

*Be with us youth in our countries, and in all Africa, and in the whole world.*

*Prepare us for the service that we should render.*

## Spiritual Prayers

*Give us hearts to understand;*

*Never to take from creation's beauty more than we give;*
*never to destroy wantonly for the furtherance of greed;*

*Never to deny to give our hands for the building of earth's beauty;*
*never to take from her what we cannot use.*

*Give us hearts to understand*
*That to destroy earth's music is to create confusion;*
*that to wreck her appearance is to blind us to beauty;*

*That to callously pollute her fragrance is to make a house of stench;*
*that as we care for her she will care for us.*

*We have forgotten who we are.*
*We have sought only our own security.*
*We have exploited simply for our own ends.*
*We have distorted our knowledge.*
*We have abused our power.*
*Great Spirit, whose dry lands thirst,*
*Help us to find the way to refresh your lands.*
*Great Spirit, whose waters are choked with debris and pollution,*
*help us to find the way to cleanse your waters.*
*Great Spirit, whose beautiful earth grows ugly with misuse,*
*help us to find the way to restore beauty to your handiwork.*
*Great Spirit, whose creatures are being destroyed,*
*help us to find a way to replenish them.*

*Great Spirit, whose gifts to us are being lost in selfishness and corruption,*
*help us to find the way to restore our humanity.*


*Oh, Great Spirit, whose voice I hear in the wind,*
*whose breath gives life to the world, hear me;*
*I need your strength and wisdom. May I walk in Beauty.*

Just as the soft rains fill the streams,
pour into the rivers, and join together in the oceans,
so may the power of every moment of your goodness
flow forth to awaken and heal all beings--
those here now, those gone before, those yet to come.

By the power of every moment of your goodness,
may your heart's wishes be soon fulfilled
as completely shining as the bright full moon,
as magically as by a wish-fulfilling gem.

By the power of every moment of your goodness,
may all dangers be averted and all disease be gone.
May no obstacle come across your way.
May you enjoy fulfillment and long life.

For all in whose heart dwells respect,
who follow the wisdom and compassion, of the Way,
may your life prosper in the four blessings
of old age, beauty, happiness and strength.

**K**eep us, O God, from pettiness;

let us be large in thought, in word, in deed.

Let us be done with faultfinding and leave off self-seeking.

May we put away all pretenses and meet each other, face to face,

without self-pity and without prejudice.

May we never be hasty in judgment and always generous.

Let us take time for all things; make us to grow calm, serene, gentle.

Teach us to put in action our better impulses-straightforward and unafraid.

Grant that we may realize it is the little things of life that create difficulties;
that in the big things of life we are as one.

Oh, Lord, let us not forget to be kind.

Amen.

## Prayer for Help

Lord God, you are everything to me. My spirit rejoices in you, my Savior. Thank you for seeking me when I was lost and for finding me. Thank you for choosing me to go forth and bear lasting fruit in your name. Thank you for enabling me to bear fruit for you, Lord. Without you, I can do nothing.

You are good, O Lord, and you are always ready to forgive. Thank you for your plentiful mercy in my life which I always receive when I call upon you. You are always there to help me; therefore, I will never be confounded. I have set my face like a flint, and I know that you will never let me be ashamed.

You truly are a very present help to me, and I am receiving your help even now as I pray. Thank you, Father. You are my refuge and strength, and because this is true, I will not fear anything or anyone.

You are in my midst, and I will not be moved. You are always there to help me speedily. You are with me, Lord. Knowing this, I will be still. I know that you are my God. Thank you for your constant help in my life, Lord.

## Hindu Prayer for the Unity of All Life

May the winds, the oceans, the herbs, and night and days,
the mother earth, the father heaven, all vegetation,
the sun, be all sweet to us.

Let us follow the path of goodness for all times,
like the sun and the moon moving eternally in the sky.

Let us be charitable to one another.
Let us not kill or be violent with one another.

Let us know and appreciate the points of view of others.
And let us unite.

May the God who is friendly, benevolent,
all-encompassing, measurer of everything, the sovereign,
the lord of speech, may He shower His blessings on us....

Oh Lord, remove my indiscretion and arrogance, control my mind.
Put an end to the snare of endless desires.
Broaden the sphere of compassion
and help me to cross the ocean of existence.

# She Who Heals – An American Indian Healing Prayer

*Mother, sing me a song That will ease my pain,*
*Mend broken bones, Bring wholeness again.*

*Catch my babies When they are born,*
*Sing my death song, Teach me how to mourn.*

*Show me the Medicine Of the healing herbs,*
*The value of spirit, The way I can serve.*

*Mother, heal my heart So that I can see*
*The gifts of yours That can live through me.*

American Indians believe that every act of life is a cycle or step on the path to healing. When we learn how to let go of our need to hold on to the past, we heal our formerly limited potential for growth. When we find courage and faith inside ourselves, we can heal our fear of future. We refuse to mentally degrade ourselves. The mind clears and allows us to be present-conscious of everything that is happening in the moment. These are all examples of healing the fragments of our lives that need to come into wholeness. When we go beyond the places where we have become numb, we feel life again. When we learn to feel again, we can heal.

# Sioux Prayer On a Voyage

You, O God, are the Lord of the mountains and the valleys.
As I travel over mountains and through valleys, I am beneath your feet.
You surround me with every kind of creature.

Peacocks, pheasants, and wild boars cross my path.
Open my eyes to see their beauty,
that I may perceive them as the work of your hands.

In your power, in your thought, all things are abundant.
Tonight I will sleep beneath your feet,
O Lord of the mountains and valleys, ruler of the trees and vines.

I will rest in your love, with you protecting me as a father protects his children,
with you watching over me as a mother watches over her children.

Then tomorrow the sun will rise and I will not know where I am;
but I know that you will guide my footsteps.

## Buddhist Morning Prayer

from the Sukhavativyuha Sutra

*Full of equanimity,*

*of benevolent thought,*

*of tender thought,*

*of affectionate thought,*

*of useful thought,*

*of serene thought,*

*of firm thought,*

*of unbiased thought,*

*of undisturbed thought,*

*of unagitated thought,*

*of thought (fixed on) the practice of discipline and transcendent wisdom,*

*having entered on knowledge which is a firm support to all thoughts,*

*equal to the ocean in wisdom,*

*equal to the mountain Meru in knowledge,*

*rich in many good qualities....*

*they attain perfect wisdom.*

Chanting of Buddhist sutras, the sacred writings that house the living voice of the Buddha, is a very common practice among the Buddhist believers in the morning. These are chanted a number of times. One radiant passage from a frequently chanted sutra, the Sukhavativyuha Sutra, describes the characteristics of true spiritual attainment:

# A Godly Meditation

Thomas More, 1478-1535

Give me grace, good Lord

To count the world as nothing,

To set my mind firmly on you

And not to hang on what people say;

To be content to be alone,

Not to long for worldly company,

Little by little to throw off the world completely

And rid my mind of all its business;

Not to long to hear of any worldly things;

Gladly to be thinking of you,

Pitifully to call for your help,

To depend on your comfort,

Busily to work to love you;

To know my own worthlessness and wretchedness,

To humble and abase myself under your mighty hand,

To lament my past sins,

To suffer adversity patiently, to purge them,

Gladly to bear my purgatory here,

To be joyful for troubles;

To walk the narrow way that leads to life,

To bear the Cross with Christ,

To keep the final hour in mind,

To have always before my eyes my death, which is always at hand,

To make death no stranger to me,

To foresee and consider the everlasting fire of hell,

To pray for pardon before the judge comes;

To keep continually in mind the passion that Christ suffered for me,

For his benefits unceasingly to give him thanks;

To buy back the time that I have wasted before,

To refrain from futile chatter,

To reject idle frivolity,

To cut out unnecessary entertainments,

To count the loss of worldly possessions, friends, liberty and life itself as absolutely nothing, for the winning of Christ;

To consider my worst enemies my best friends,

For Joseph's brothers could never have done him as much good with their love and favor as they did with their malice and hatred.

## Prayer For Deliverance

My Lord, You are all powerful, You are God, you are Father.

We beg you through the intercession and help of the archangels Michael, Raphael, and Gabriel, for the deliverance of our brothers and sisters who are enslaved by the evil one. All saints of heaven, come to our aid.

From anxiety, sadness, and obsessions,
We beg You. Free us, O Lord.

From hatred, fornication, envy,
We beg You. Free us, O Lord.

From thoughts of jealousy, rage, and death.
We beg You. Free us, O Lord.

From every thought of suicide and abortion.
We beg You.

From the onslaught of this sniper, we beg You:
Free us, O Lord.

From every form of sinful sexuality. We beg You.
Free us, O Lord.

From every division in our family, and every harmful friendship.
We beg You. Free us, O Lord.

From every sort of spell, malice, witchcraft, and every form of the occult and homicide. We beg You. Free us, O Lord.

Lord, You who said, "I leave you peace, my peace I give you," grant that, through the intercession of the Virgin Mary, we may be liberated from every evil spell and enjoy Your peace always.

In the name of Christ, our Lord. Amen.

# Illumination for the Dead

**A** simple ritual, called an *Illumination,* is usually performed following the dead of a family member, closed friend or of a relative. The glasses on the Boveda are arranged to create a pyramid. This means that 3 glasses are placed in a row next to each other. On top of those are set 2 more glasses. On top of this 'pile' is set the 6th glass. The large glass is then placed in front of this construction.

A white 7 day candle is lit on the Boveda and an additional glass of water is also places in it. Sometimes, people will write the name of the diseased person on a piece of paper which is the places, facing up, under the glass. It is best to put the additional glass and the candle on a white plate!

Every day, for 7 days, these prayers are repeated and the plate with the glass and the candle are 'raised' higher. This is simply done by putting a book underneath. In this way the candle and glass will be raised higher each day and we pray that the spirit of the diseased person will illuminate itself and be able to find peace and tranquility in the afterlife and will be able to let go of all earthly boundaries.

This simple but effective ritual is accompanied by Prayers for the Dead which can be found from page 71 of this book.

# ABOUT THE AUTHOR

## Mario dos Ventos
Macumbeiro/Espiritista

Afro-Brazilian & Afro-Caribbean
Shamanism, Healing & Witchcraft
Psychic Readings & Consultations

phone: +44 (0) 7804 444 794
email: Casa_dos_Ventos@hotmail.co.uk
web: www.exu.moonfruit.com

**Mario dos Ventos** lives in Surrey, United Kingdom. He is an internationally renowned Macumbeiro, trained Spirit Medium and Spiritual Worker. He has trained with practitioners and initiates of Brazilian Umbanda & Quimbanda, Southern Style Hoodoo & Rootwork as well as Puerto Rican and Caribbean Spiritism and Bujeria.

Mario has published articles for various spiritual periodicals and magazines, and has given talks on Afro-Brazilian Magic and Witchcraft at a number of conferences and gatherings. He teaches courses and workshops on Spiritual Development, Divination, Plant Lore, African-based Witchcraft and Magic, Brazilian Umbanda and The Magical Powers of the Saints.

He works as a freelance spiritual reader and advisor for *Erzulie's UK*, the European branch of New Orleans' finest botanica and is one of the columnists of *Mystic Pop Magazine*.

Mario is internationally available for Lenormand Card Readings and consultations with the Brazilian Nkobo Shell divination system (a variation of the Brazilian jogo de búzios), and provides are variety of spiritual services to clients all over Europe, North & South America and Asia.

His personal web page is **www.exu.moonfruit.com**

He can be contacted on: **casa_dos_ventos@hotmail.co.uk**

## SARAVA UMBANDA
### The Inner Workings of Macumba

Drawing on the teachings and practices of different Umbanda Temples in Brazil, this landmark book, which contains 44 chapters, spread over more then 420 pages, explain the history, cosmology and theology of Umbanda, look at ceremonies, the organizational structure of individual centers and the pantheon of this religion.

This book also explains Umbanda Initiation, the 'necklaces of the worshipers', gives recipes for special workings for cleansings, prosperity, luck, love and happiness.

A special part of this book is also dedicated to the application of Umbanda outside of Brazil. What new challenges must be faced and how can we adapt without compromising the roots, values and believes of Umbanda?

440 pages, 8.50" x 11.00"

## THE GAME OF DESTINY
### Fortune Telling with Lenormand Cards

The most comprehensive book ever published on the Fortune Telling Cards of Mlle Lenormand, *The Game of Destiny* contains the meanings of all 36 cards, card combinations, special meanings and several different spreads of this unique divination system.

Known in Brazil as *O Baralho Cigano*, the Gypsy Deck, the cards that this book deals with have long been employed by many followers of Umbanda and Quimbanda/Macumba to read the future and gain insights into the workings of the spirit world.

An extra chapter on how to invoke the aid of the Gypsy Spirits in card divination and instructions and recipes to aid clients and readers alike make this book an exceptionally valuable guide for beginners and professional readers alike.

208 pages, 8.50" x 11.00"

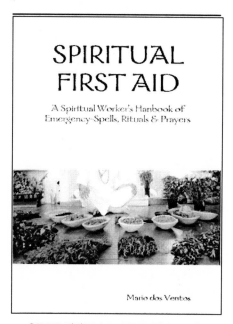

**SPIRITUAL FIRST AID**
**A Spiritual Worker's Handbook**
**of Emergency-Spells, Rituals & Prayers**

A quick and easy to use 'Spiritual Emergency Tool', this gem contains spells calling upon God, gods and goddesses, saints and sinners. Spiritual Cleansings and Revocations, spells and rituals to overcome depression, anxiety and a broken heart, tips and tricks to boost your Psychic Protection and how to quickly invoke a Spiritual Bodyguard are just some of the useful works that this book provides.

Chock full of magical incantations, quick recipes, spells, prayers and other treasures of Spiritual Emergency Help, this gold mine of information should not be missing from any Spiritual Worker's bookshelf. The extended appendix also provides ideas and recipes for a 'Spiritual Emergency Kit'.

184 pages, 6.00" x 9.00"